Living In

The

Spirit Realm

What We Will Encounter

in Heaven

William J. Morford

True Potential
REACH THE WORLD

Cover and Interior page design by True Potential, Inc.

ISBN: (paperback): 9781953247964
ISBN: (e-book): 9781953247971
LCCN: 2022948565

True Potential, Inc.
PO Box 904, Travelers Rest, SC 29690
www.truepotentialmedia.com
Printed in the United States of America.

Contents

INTRODUCTION

Living in the Spirit Realm is immediately preceded by moving into the Spirit Realm!

> Joel 3:4. *The sun will be turned into darkness and the moon into blood, before the great and the terrible Day of the LORD* comes. (Revelation 6:12) 5. And it will be (that) whoever calls on the name of the LORD* will be delivered, for deliverance will be in Mount Zion and in Jerusalem, as the LORD* has said, and in the **remnant** whom the LORD* will call.* (John 6:44, Acts 2:17-21, Romans 10:13)

The **Remnant** is those who have walked in **Repentance** as ordered by **Y'shua** in Matthew 4:17. These are the **Humble** who have the mark of the man with the Inkhorn, in Ezekiel 9:4.

Valley of Jehoshaphat

> Joel 4.1. *For, behold, in those days, and in that time, when I shall bring back the **captivity** of Judah and Jerusalem, 2. I shall also gather all the nations (heathens) and will bring them down into the **Valley of Jehoshaphat**, and will plead with them there for **My people** and for **My heritage Israel**, whom they have scattered among the nations, and parted My land. 3. And they have cast lots for **My people** and have given a boy for a harlot, and sold a girl for wine, so they could drink.*

The **Valley of Jehoshaphat** is a few miles southeast of Jerusalem, called the **Valley of Beracha** in 2 Chronicles 20:26. This is the battle in Revelation

20:7, culminating in the **destruction of Gog & Magog** by **fire** from **heaven**. God zaps the enemies of Israel, taking complete control over the final battle; with this **victory,** the solar system is dissolved, ending **Judgment Day**, which lasted an unknown number of years.

> Joel 4:4. *Yes, and what have you to do with Me, O Tyre and Sidon and all the districts of Philistia? Will you repay Me? And if you pay Me back, I shall swiftly and speedily return your pay back upon your own head 5. because you have taken My silver and My gold, and have car-*ried ***My goodly treasures into your palaces.*** *6. You have also* ***sold the children of Judah*** *and the* ***children of Jerusalem*** *to the sons of the Greeks, so you could remove them far from their border. 7. Behold,* ***I shall raise them out of the place where you have sold them and will return your pay back upon your own head.*** *8. And I shall sell your sons and your daughters into the hand of the children of* ***Judah***, *and they will sell them to the (people of Sheba), to nations far off, for the LORD* has spoken it.*

The LORD* has taken the children of Israel into Heaven, to ETERNAL LIFE.

> Joel 4:9. *Proclaim this among the* ***nations,*** ***Prepare war***, *wake up the mighty men, let all the men of war draw near! They will come up! 10. Beat your plowshares into swords and your pruning hooks into spears. Let the weak say, I am strong! 11. Make haste and come, all you* ***nations*** *around about, and gather yourselves together there.*
>
> ***Cause Your mighty ones*** *to come down,* ***LORD****.

The **Nations** are all Heathens, preparing for War, which will never take place because God zaps them with **fire**! The LORD* of Hosts comes, bringing **Fire** that destroys every enemy of Himself and Israel!

> Joel 4:12. *Let the* ***nations*** *be awakened and come up to the* ***Valley of Jehoshaphat***, *for there I shall sit to* ***judge*** *all the* ***nations*** *around about. 13. Put in the sickle, for the* ***harvest*** *is ripe. Come, get yourself down, for the* ***wine press*** *is full, the vats overflow, for their* ***wickedness*** *is great. (Revelation 14:15; 19:15)*

*Revelation 14:15. Then another **angel** came out of the Sanctuary crying in a loud voice to the One Who was sitting on the cloud, "You must now send your sickle and you must now **reap**, because the time to **reap** has come, because the **harvest of the earth has withered.**"*

The LORD* has been **patient**, giving everyone time to repent.

*Revelation 19:15. And a **large sharp sword** was going out of His mouth, (Isa. 49:2) so that with it He could slaughter the heathens, and He will shepherd them with an iron rod, (Ps. 2:9) and He treads the wine press (Isa. 63:3, Jl. 3:13, Lam. 1:15) of the wine of the burning wrath of the God of Hosts, 16. and He has upon His garment, even **over** His thigh a name that has been written: "**King of Kings and Lord of Lords.**"*

The **large, sharp sword** was the strongest personal weapon in ancient times, with The **Word of God** still the most powerful weapon we have. Notice that His title, "**King of Kings and Lord of Lords,**" is over His thigh, written on His garment.

*Joel 4:14. Multitudes, multitudes in the **Valley of Decision**, for the **Day of the LORD*** is near in the **Valley of Decision**. 15. The sun and the moon will be **darkened**, and the **stars** will withdraw their **shining**. (Revelation 6:13; 8:12) 16. The **LORD*** also will roar out of **Zion** and utter His voice from **Jerusalem** and the **heavens** and the **earth** will **shake**, but the **LORD*** will be a **refuge** for **His people** and the **stronghold of the children of Israel**. 17. So you will know that I AM the LORD* your God, dwelling in Zion, My holy mountain: then Jerusalem will be holy, and no strangers will pass through there anymore.*

This is another description of the End of Judgment Day, with the sun and moon darkened; the People of the LORD* are safely taken in **ETERNAL LIFE**, the earth **shaken**, **destroyed**, and the strangers, Heathens, sent to the Second Death! God zaps His enemies, who are the enemies of His People, Israel.

*Joel 4:18. And it will be in that **Day**, the mountains will drop down new wine and the hills will flow with **milk** and all the **rivers of Judah*** *will flow with waters and a fountain will come forth from the House of the LORD* and will water the **Valley of Shittim**. (Rev. 22:1) 19. Egypt will be a desolation and Edom will be a desolate wilderness, because of the **violence (against)** the children of **Judah**, because they (Egypt and Edom) have shed innocent blood in their land. 20. But **Judah** will **dwell forever** and **Jerusalem** from generation to generation. 21. For I shall cleanse their blood (that) I have not cleansed, and then the **LORD*** will dwell (forever) in **Zion**.*

The **LORD*** dwells forever in **Heaven**, where **we shall join Him** as each one graduates into the Spirit Realm. Joel chapter four is an allegory, bringing us into the **LORD*'s** and **Y'shua's** domain, the Ultimate destination for each believer. This book gives some idea of what each of us will encounter in Heaven.

WHAT THE SPIRIT REALM IS LIKE

1

Living in the Spirit Realm will be very different from life as we know it in the here and now. There will be nothing physical, yet everything will be real! Our bodies will not be physical; we will not breathe, will not require natural food, and will not require sleep or rest. We will not have vocal cords, eardrums, or eyes, yet we will sing and hear and see! How can this be?

There will be no sun or moon, with time being a new dimension. All this newness is explored in this book, helping us to appreciate what is coming. So, enjoy this exploration into the unknown, pulling on the Bible and other sources to help us understand what we do not know - how different life will be.

Our Spirit Bodies will look like our Earthly Bodies, so we will recognize our friends and public figures. Those who have had visits to Heaven tell us everyone looks to be about thirty years old, an extra blessing from the LORD*! When God has come to Earth, He has come as a man, evidence of our being made in His image.

> Genesis 1:26. *Then God said,* **"We will make mankind in our image, after our likeness and have dominion over the fish of the sea, over the fowl of the air, over the cattle, over all the earth, and over every creeping thing that creeps upon the earth."** 27. *So God created* **mankind** *in His own image; He created him in the* **image of God**. *He created them* **male and female**.

Mankind has been made in the image of God, as is seen whenever God has appeared on Earth as He appeared to Abraham:

> Genesis 18:1. ***And the LORD* appeared*** *to him in the plains of Mamre and he was sitting in the tent door in the heat of the day. 2. And he lifted up his eyes and looked, and **there were three men standing by him**. And when he saw them, he ran from the tent door to meet them and he bowed toward the ground 3. and said, "My Lord, if now I have found favor in Your sight, do not pass by, I pray **You**, from **Your** servant: 4. let a little water, I pray you, be brought and wash your feet and rest yourselves under the tree. 5. And I shall get a morsel of bread and comfort your hearts for you. After that you will pass on, for that is why you have come to your servant." And they said, "So do as you have said." 6. And Abraham hastened into the tent to Sarah and said, "Make ready quickly three measures of fine meal, knead it and make cakes." 7. And Abraham ran to the herd and fetched a good, tender calf and gave it to a young man and he hastened to dress it. 8. And he took butter, milk, and the calf which he had dressed and set it before them, and he stood by them under the tree and they ate.*

The **Living God** appeared as a **man**, the same as when **He** appeared as **Y'shua**, proving that we are made in **His image**. In verse three above, **You** and **Your** are capitalized because they are singular, referring specifically to God, showing that **Abraham** knew he was being visited by **God**. The other two visitors were **angels**, who also looked like men; we are made in His image! We also are made in His emotional image, having the same emotions that God has!

These Spirit men had attributes of physical men when they were in the physical world. They could eat, and appear to be natural, physical men. They left Abraham and went down to visit Lot to lead his family out of Sodom.

> Genesis 19.1. *And **two angels** came to **Sodom** in the evening and **Lot** was sitting in the gate of Sodom. And when **Lot** saw them he rose up to meet them and he bowed himself with his face toward the ground. 2. And he said, "Behold now, my lords, turn in, I pray you, into your servant's house and tarry all night and wash your feet and*

you will rise up early and go on your way." And they said, "No. But we will stay in the street all night." 3. And he pressed upon them greatly and they went in with him and entered his house and he made a feast for them and baked unleavened bread and they ate.

The **Angels** had to be persuaded by **Lot** to come to his house for the night, although they surely knew the wickedness of **Sodom**. This shows that they appear as normal human beings until they exhibit supernatural power, striking the men of Sodom with blindness.

Genesis 19:4. *But before they lay down, the **men** of the city, the **men** of Sodom, surrounded the house, both old and young, all the people from every quarter. 5. And they called to **Lot** and said to him, "Where are the **men** who came in to you tonight? **Bring them out to us**, so we can **know** them." 6. And **Lot** went out to them at the door and shut the door behind him 7. and said, "I pray you, brothers, do not behave so **wickedly**. 8. Behold now, I have two daughters who have not known a man: let me, I pray you, bring them out to you and you do to them as is good in your eyes. Only to these **men** do nothing, for therefore they came under the shadow of my roof." 9. And they said, **"Stand back!"** And they said again, "This one came in to sojourn and he thinks he is a judge. Now **we** will deal worse with **you** than with **them**." And they pressed sore upon the man, **Lot**, and came near to break the door. 10. But the **men (angels)** put forth their hand and pulled **Lot** into the house to them and shut the door. 11. And **they** struck the **men (Sodomites)** with **blindness** that were at the door of the house, both small and great, so that they wearied themselves to find the door. 12. And the **men (Angels)** said to **Lot**, "Do you have here any besides yourself? Sons-in-law, your sons, your daughters, and whoever you have in the city, bring them out of this place, 13. for **we will destroy this place**, because their cry has become great before the face of the **LORD***, and the **LORD*** has sent **us to destroy it**."*

The **Angels** were strong enough to rescue **Lot** from the grasp of the mob, then strike the entire mob with blindness. The power of the **Angels** allowed them to call down the fire and brimstone that destroyed the most wicked cities.

Genesis 19:14. *And **Lot** went out and spoke to his **sons-in-law**, who **married** his daughters, and said, "Get up, get out of this place, for the LORD* will destroy this city." But he seemed like one who teased to his **sons-in-law**. 15. And when the morning came, then the **angels** hastened Lot saying, "Arise, take your wife and your two daughters that are here, so you will not be consumed in the **iniquity** of the city." 16. And while he lingered, the **men** laid hold upon his hand and upon the hand of his wife and upon the hand of his two daughters. The **LORD*** had pity on him and they brought him out and set him outside the city. 17. And it was, when they had brought them out, that he said, "Escape for your life! **Do not look behind you! Do not stay anywhere in the plain!** Escape to the mountain, so you will not be consumed." 18. And Lot said to them, "Oh, **not so**, my lord. 19. Behold now your servant has found favor in your sight and you have magnified your **loving kindness**, which you have shown to me in saving my life. And I cannot escape to the mountain, lest something evil overtake me and I die. 20. Behold now, this city is near to flee to and it is a little one. Oh, let me escape there, (is it not a **little one**?) and my soul will live." 21. And he said to him, "See, I have accepted you concerning this thing also, that I shall not overthrow this city of which you have spoken. 22. Quick! Escape there, for I cannot do anything until you have come there." Therefore the name of the city was called **Zoar**.*

Although the two young men are called sons-in-law, they were just engaged. The Jewish marriage was considered complete at the official engagement, although the marriage would not be consummated for some time, often a year or more. The **name** of the **Little City**, **Zoar,** means **Insignificant**.

Genesis 19:23. *The sun had risen upon the earth when **Lot** entered **Zoar**. 24. Then the **LORD*** rained **brimstone** and **fire** from the LORD* out of heaven upon Sodom and upon Gomorrah.*

All the **Sinners** were killed! Showing that they were entering the **Second Death!**

JUDGMENT

2

Entry to the Spirit Realm is through Repentance, which makes you Righteous.

> Leviticus 18.1. *And the **LORD*** spoke to Moses, saying, 2. "Speak to the children of Israel and say to them,*
>
> *"I am the **LORD*** **your God**. 3. You will not do after the doings of the land of Egypt in which you dwelled, and after the doings of the land of Canaan where I bring you, you will not do. Neither will you walk in their ordinances. 4. You will do **My judgments** and keep **My ordinances**, to walk in them, I AM the LORD* your God. 5. You will therefore keep My statutes and My judgments, which if a man does he will live in them. I AM the LORD*.*

The **LORD*** yearns for relationship with each individual, so all mankind would **ENTER LIFE**, meaning make it to Heaven. People tend to focus on what is called the Ten Commandments, but Leviticus chapter eighteen lists many more than ten commandments, while other chapters in Leviticus and other books detail many things that have to be followed by believers. Only the **Righteous** will be taken to Heaven, as marked by the Man with the Inkhorn in Ezekiel Nine. Y'shua in Matthew 4:17 says to walk continuously in **Repentance**. That is the only way each believer can cover every sin.

> Matthew 25:31. *"And when the **Son of Man** would come in **His glory** and all the angels with Him, (Deut. 33:2) then **He** will sit upon*

*the **Throne of His Glory**: 32. and all the multitudes will be gathered in front of Him, and **He** will **separate** them from one another, as the shepherd **separates** the **sheep** from the **goats**, 33. then indeed **He** will place the **sheep** on **His right hand**, but the **goats** on **His left**.*

The **throne** of the **King** of the **Universe** is made of the **Glory of His Presence**. Jeremiah 14:21 speaks of the **Throne of Your Glory,** and Jewish commentary has many references to **Throne of Glory**. Matthew 19:28 also has **Throne of His Glory**.

The **right hand** here is a symbol of **God's salvation**, from Psalm 20:7. *Now I know that the **LORD*** saves **His** anointed. **He** will hear him from **His Holy Heaven** with the saving strength of **His Right Hand**,* while the **left** symbolizes **calamity and judgment**. See Right Hand in Glossary.

The Judgment at the Great White Throne

Revelation 20:11. *Then I saw a **Great White Throne** and the **One Who sits upon it**, from **Whose presence** the earth (Psalm 114:3,7) and the **sky** fled and a **place was not found** for them. 12. Then I saw the **dead**, the great and the small, **standing before** the **throne**. And **scrolls** were **opened**, and another **scroll** was **opened**, which is of **life**, (Exod. 32:32,33, Ps. 69:29, Dan. 12:1) and the **dead** were **judged** according to their **deeds**, (Isa. 59:18, Jer. 17:10, Ps. 28:4; 62:13, Pro. 24:12, Rom. 2:6, 1 Cor. 3:8) by what had been written in the **scrolls**. (Dan. 7:9,10) 13. Then the sea gave up the **dead** that were in it and **Death** and **Hades** gave up the **dead**, those in them, and **each** was **judged** according to his **works**. 14. Then **Death** and **Hades** were **thrown violently** into the **Lake of Fire**. This is the **Second Death**, the **Lake of Fire**. 15. And if someone was not found written in the **Book of Life**, he was cast into the **Lake of Fire**.*

Verse fourteen cites the sinners being thrown **violently into the Lake of Fire!**

Isaiah 30:27. *Behold, the **name of the LORD*** comes from afar, burning (with) **His anger** and in a thick cloud of smoke. **His** lips are full of **indignation** and **His** tongue is a **consuming fire**. 28. And*

*His breath is like an overflowing stream. It will reach to the midst of the neck, to sift the **nations (Heathens)** with the sieve of vanity and there will be a bridle in the jaws of the people, causing (them) to err. 29. You will have a song, as in the night when a festival is sanctified, and gladness of heart, as when one goes with a flute to come to the mountain of the **LORD***, to the **Mighty One of Israel**. 30. And the **LORD*** will cause His glorious voice to be heard and will show the lightning down from **His** arm with the **indignation** of (**His**) **anger**, and (with) the **flame** of a **consuming fire**, (accompanied by) crashing and tempest and hailstones. 31. For through the **voice of the LORD*** Assyria will be beaten down, struck with a rod. 32. And in every place where the appointed staff will pass, which the **LORD*** will lay upon him, it will be with drums and harps and in battles of shaking He will fight with it. 33. For **Tafteh** was ordained of old. Yes, it is prepared for the (Assyrian) king, He has made it deep and large. Its pile is **fire** and lots of **wood**: the **breath of the LORD***, like a stream of **brimstone**, kindles it.*

The **Breath of the LORD*** at the **Great White Throne Judgment** in Revelation will be just as it was against ancient Assyria. **Tafteh** is named in 2 Kings 22:3 and in Jeremiah 7:31 as a place where human sacrifices were burned. Those who committed that atrocity will be burned in the Lake of Fire of the **Second Death**.

Exodus 32:33. *And the **LORD*** said to Moses, "**Whoever has sinned against Me, I shall erase from My book....**"*

There will be no unbelievers in Heaven. But what about those unrighteous leaders who go to be with their Fathers when they die? They wait, asleep in death, for the **final Judgment**, which comes during the **Great White Throne Judgment** that goes on for a **long time** when the LORD* sends the six men in Ezekiel 9: The **Long Time** takes place during **Judgment Day**, explained in "Glimpses into the Spirit Realm" by this author. **Judgment Day** is not one twenty-four-hour day like we have now, but Judgment takes a long time.

Ezekiel 9:1. *Then He cried in my ears with a loud voice saying, Cause those who have charge over the city to draw near, even every man* *(with) his destroying weapon in his hand. 2. And, behold, **six men** came from the road of the higher gate, which lies toward the north and each man a slaughter weapon in his hand, and **one man** among them was clothed with **linen**, with a **writer's inkhorn** by his side. And they went in and stood beside the bronze altar. 3. And the **glory** of the **God of Israel** went up from the cherub, upon which it was, to the threshold of the House. And He called to the man clothed in **linen**, who (had) the **writer's inkhorn** by his side.*

Ezekiel 9 is detailed in the chapter, THE WONDERFUL ATMOSPHERE IN HEAVEN.

Messiah

Malachi 3.1. *Behold, I am sending **My messenger** and he will pre-pare the **Way before Me**, (Mark 1:2, Luke 1:76; 7:27) and the **Lord Whom you seek** will come suddenly to **His Temple**, even the mes-senger of the covenant, in **Whom you delight**. Behold, **He will come**, says the LORD* of Hosts. 2. But who can abide the **Day** of His coming?! (Revelation 6:17) Who will stand when He appears?! For **He** is like a **refiner's fire** and like **fullers' soap**. 3. And **He** will sit (as) a **refiner** and **purifier** of silver, and **He** will **purify** the **sons of Levi** and **purge** those like **gold** and **silver**, and then they will offer an offering in **acts of loving kindness** to the LORD*. 4. Then the offer-ing of Judah and Jerusalem will be pleasing to the LORD*, as in the days of old, and as in former years. 5. And **I shall come near to you for judgment**, and I shall be a swift witness against the **sorcerers** and against the **adulterers** and against **false swearers** and against those who **oppress the worker** in his wages, the **widow** and the **fatherless**, and (all) who turn aside the stranger from his right, and **do not revere Me**, says the LORD* of Hosts.*

The **Lord Y'shua and the LORD* of Hosts are One and the Same!** The **Two** Who are **One** come on **Judgment Day** to judge the **Quick** and the **Dead**. **Saints** will be purged and declared **Righteous** during **Judgment Day**. The **Sons of Levi** are those who have been declared **Righteous**, all Jewish and non-Jewish. The non-Jewish **Saint** has been grafted in, so everyone is Jewish. Romans 11:19. *"Therefore you will say, 'Branches were* *broken off so that I could be grafted in."* After purging, each **Saint** will continuously offer **Acts of Loving Kindness."**

Psalm 1:5. *Therefore the **ungodly will <u>not</u> stand in the judgment, nor will sinners in the congregation of the righteous**. 6. For the **LORD*** knows the **Way of the righteous**, but **the way of the ungodly will perish**.*

The **Ungodly** will not Enter Life, **ETERNAL LIFE!**

Psalm 9:8. *But the **LORD*** will endure forever. He has prepared **His throne** for **judgment**. 9. And **He will judge the world in righteousness**, He will **minister judgment** to the people in uprightness.*

Matthew 12:36. *And I say to **you** that every idle word which men will speak will be paid back with regard to his account on **Judgment Day**: 37. for **you** will be **justified, declared righteous**, because of **your words**, and **you** will be **condemned because of your words**."*

Each **you** in verses 36 and 37 is singular, showing that **you** are responsible for **your** fate! Remember, **Judgment Day** lasts a very long time! See the last chapter in Glimpses into the Spirit Realm.

Matthew 12:42. *(The) **Queen of the South** will rise in **the judgment** with this generation and will condemn it, because she came from the ends of the Earth to hear the wisdom of Solomon, and behold (One) greater than Solomon is here."*

The **Queen of the South** is the Queen of Sheba. **The judgment** refers to Judgment Day.

Ishmael was gathered to his people, which would later include all those named below:

Genesis 25:12. *Now these are the generations of **Ishmael**, **Abraham's son** whom Hagar the Egyptian, Sarah's handmaid, bore to **Abraham**. 13. And these are the names of the sons of **Ishmael**, by their names according to their generations: the firstborn of **Ishmael**, Nebaioth, Kedar, Adbeel, Mibsham, 14. Mishma, Dumah, Massa, 15. Hadad,*

*Tema, Jetur, Nafish, and Kedemah. 16. These are the sons of **Ishmael** and these are their names, by their towns and by their small villages; twelve princes according to their tribes. 17. And these are the years of the **life of Ishmael**, a **hundred thirty-seven years**, and **he expired** and **died** and was **gathered to his people**. 18. And they dwelled from Havilah to Shur that is before Egypt, as you go toward Assyria: he died in the presence of all his brothers.*

"**Gathered to his people**" may not include his father, Abraham since it is not expected for Ishmael to get to Heaven because of his antipathy to **Isaac**. **Abraham** would have been among Ishmael's people. The **separation** of the Good from the Bad comes at the **Great White Throne Judgment**, the very final act of **Judgment!**

UnGodly kings were joined to their fathers, which included some **evil kings**, meaning that **Ishmael** being gathered to his people would have been with the good and the bad until the Final Judgment.

1 Kings 14:20. *And the days which **Jeroboam** reigned were twenty-two years and **he slept with his fathers**, and Nadab his son reigned in his stead.*

Jeroboam was a sinner but slept with his **Fathers** until the final **Judgment!**

1 Kings 15:8. *And **Abijam** slept with his fathers and they buried him in the city of David and Asa his son reigned in his stead.*

Abijam was a sinner who put prostitutes and idols in hilltop shrines, then slept with his fathers until **Judgment Day**.

1 Kings 15:11. *And **Asa** did that which was right in the eyes of the LORD*, like **David** his father. 12. And he **took away the prosti-tutes, (both male and female), from the land and removed all the idols** that his **fathers had made**. 13. And also **Maacah his mother**; he even removed her from being queen because **she had made an idol in a grove**, and **Asa destroyed and burned her idol** by the brook Kidron. 14. But the high places were not removed. Nevertheless **Asa's heart was faithful with the LORD*** all his days. 15. And he brought*

in the things which his father had dedicated and the things which he himself had dedicated into the House of the LORD*, silver, gold, and vessels.

Asa was a righteous king.

1 Kings 15:23b *But in the time of his old age he was diseased in his feet. 24. And **Asa slept with his fathers**, and was **buried with his fathers** in the city of **David** his father and **Jehoshaphat** his son reigned in his stead.*

When **Asa** slept with his fathers, the **fathers** included the bad ancestors as well as the good. What happens after that is **Judgment Day**, **the Great White Throne Judgment** when the sheep and the goats are separated.

Matthew 25:31. *"And when the Son of Man would come in His glory and all the angels with Him, (Deut. 33:2) then He will sit upon (the) **Throne of His Glory**: 32. and all the multitudes will be gathered in front of Him, and He will **separate them from one another**, as the **shepherd separates the sheep from the goats**, 33. then indeed **He** will place the **sheep on His right hand**, but the **goats on His left**. 34. Then the King will say to those on **His right hand**, '**Come, the blessed of My Father, you must now inherit what has been prepared for you (in the) kingdom** from the foundation of the world. 35. For I was hungry and you gave Me to eat, I was thirsty and you gave Me to drink, I was a stranger and you took Me in, 36. and I was poorly clothed and you clothed Me, I was sick and you visited Me, I was in prison and you came to Me.' 37. Then the righteous will answer Him saying, 'Lord, when did we see You hungry and we fed You, or thirsty and we gave (You something) to drink? 38. And when did we see You a stranger and we took You in, or poorly clothed and we clothed You? 39. And when did we see You sick or in prison and we came to You?' 40. Then the King will say to them, 'Truly I say to you, in so much as you did (anything) for one of these, the least of My brothers, you did (it) for **Me**.'* (Isaiah 58:6-10)

The **throne** of the **King of the Universe** is made of the **Glory of His Presence**. Jeremiah 14:21 speaks of the **Throne of Your Glory,** and Jewish commentary has many references to **Throne of Glory**. Matthew 19:28 also has **Throne of His Glory**. The **right hand** here is a symbol of **God's salvation**, from Psalm 20:6, while the **left** symbolizes **calamity** and **judgment**. The **separation** in verse thirty-three happens at the end of **Judgment Day**, so all those who slept with their fathers joined the **good** and the **bad** until the end of time when **Judgment Day** comes, and they (the **good**) are **separated** from those who were **bad**. In verse thirty-six, The Greek word for clothed refers to the **outer garment**, the **prayer shawl**. Verse forty gives the **real Heart of God**, to **Love your Neighbor as Yourself**, Leviticus 19:18.

> 1 Kings 16.1. *Then the word of the LORD* came to Jehu the son of Hanani against* **Basha** *saying, 2. Forasmuch as I raised you out of the dust and made you prince over My people Israel, and you have walked in the way of* **Jeroboam and have made My people Israel to sin**, *to* **provoke Me to anger with their sins**, *3. behold, I shall remove* **Basha** *and his house, and will make* **your house** *like the* **house of Jeroboam** *the son of Nebat. 4. He of* **Basha** *who dies in the city the dogs will eat, and he who dies in the fields the fowls of the air will eat. 5. Now the rest of the acts of Basha and what he did and his might, are they not written in the Book of the Chronicles of the Kings of Israel? 6. So* **Basha slept with his fathers** *and was buried in Tirzah, and Elah his son reigned in his stead.*

Basha slept with his fathers, who were sinners. They all would end up in the **Lake of Fire**, the **Second Death**. **Judgment Day** will take care of those who do not **Repent**.

> Luke 23:39. *Then one of the evil ones who was hanging there was blaspheming Him saying, "Are You not the* **Messiah**? *You must now save* **Yourself** *and* **us**." *40. But the* **other** *said, rebuking him, "Do you not yourself* **fear God**, *because you are in the same sentence? 41. But we indeed justly, for what we did is worthy (of what) we are receiving: but this* **One** *did nothing improper." 42. Then he was saying,* **"Y'shua, You must right away remember me when You would enter Your Kingdom."** *43. Then He said to him,* **"Truly I say to you, <u>this very day you will be with Me in Paradise."</u>**

It is apparent from this and from Paul's statement in 2 Corinthians 5 that there may not be any waiting for the end of **Judgment Day** to enter **Heaven**, **Paradise**, but, alternatively, **since there is no time in the Spirit Realm,** that becomes a **moot point.**

> 2 Corinthians 5:6. *Therefore, since we are always confident, and knowing that when we are at home in the body we are getting away from the Lord: 7. because we are walking by faith, not by sight: 8. but we are confident;* **we even rather prefer to leave from the body and to be <u>at home with the Lord</u>**. *9. For this reason then we strive earnestly, whether when we are at home or when we are away, to be well pleasing to Him.*

The above verse indicates that the time between death and presence in Heaven will be very short. That is because when anyone who leaves the physical body is instantly in the **Spirit Realm**, where time does not exist, so there will not be any sense of time between entering the **Spirit Realm** and observing the entire **Spirit Realm**. The many kings of Israel and Judah who were then with their fathers until being judged, then they either went to Heaven or to the Second Death. The prevailing Christian view is that only believers in Y'shua go to Heaven, but how about **Abraham**? How about **Isaac**? How about **Jacob**? How about **David**? How about **Y'shua's** statements, "The **Father** and **I** are **One**." and "The one who has seen **Me** has seen the **Father**:" **Abraham** and his household saw **God**. **Moses** and the **Elders** saw **God** on the mountain. Christians believe that **Abraham** and **Moses** are in **Heaven**, so why not other **Jews,** including all the **Patriarchs**? Then, why not the **martyrs** of the **Holocaust**?

> Genesis 35:27. *And Jacob came to Isaac, his father in Mamre,* **Kiri-at-Arba** *which is Hebron, where Abraham and Isaac lived. 28. And the days of Isaac were a hundred eighty years. 29. And* **Isaac expired** *and* **died** *and was* **gathered to his people,** *being old and full of days: and his sons* **Esau** *and* **Jacob** *buried him.*

This is still another indication that the time between death and being in the **Spirit Realm** will be very short. In verse twenty-seven, **Kiriat** means any walled city.

Jeremiah 8:12. *Were they ashamed when they had committed abominations? No, they were not at all ashamed, nor could they blush. Therefore they will fall among those who fall. They will be cast down in the* **time of their visitation***, says the LORD*.*

Throughout the Bible, in both the **Hebrew Text** and the **Greek, Visitation** refers to the time of **Punishment,** meaning **Judgment Day**. Most often, it is translated as **Visitation**, but occasionally **Punishment**, which is an alternative meaning.

People Do Not Know Judgment of the LORD*:

Jeremiah 8:4. *Moreover you will say to them, Thus says the LORD*,* **Will they fall and not rise? Will He turn away and not return?** *5. Why then has this people of Jerusalem slid back by a perpetual backsliding? They hold fast deceit, they* **refuse to return***, (repent). 6. I listened and heard, (but) they did not speak aright.* **No one repented** *of his wickedness saying, What have I done? Each person thinks he is perfect, so everyone turns away in his course, like a horse that rushes in the battle. 7. Yes, the stork in the sky knows her appointed times and the turtle and the crane and the swallow observe the time of their coming, but* **My people do not know the judgment of the LORD***. *8. How do you say, We are wise and the Torah (Instruction) of the LORD* is with us? See, He certainly made it in vain. The pen of the scribes is in vain. 9. The* **wise are ashamed, they are dismayed and taken***. See, they have* **rejected** *the* **word of the LORD*** *and what wisdom is in them?*

Christians and Jews alike think that just because they go to Church or Synagogue, they automatically have a pass to Heaven, but as **Y'shua** said, *"You must* **continuously Repent** *for the Kingdom of the Heavens has drawn near."* Each **individual Walking** in **Repentance** is the **key**; nothing else will do! Each **individual** is **judged on his own**; no one else can do that for you, and you cannot substitute for anyone else. It is a **heart** condition that gets you **into Heaven** or keeps you **out** of **Heaven**.

Jeremiah 10:6. *Since there is no one like You, LORD*, Your name is Great and Your name is Great in Might. 7.* **Who would not revere**

*You, King of the Nations! (Rev. 15:4) For to You only does it pertain, since among all the wise men of the nations and in all their kingdoms there is no one like You. 8. But through one thing they are brutish and foolish, the stock is a doctrine of **vanities**. 9. Silver spread onto plates is brought from Tarshish and gold from Ufaz, the work of the workman and of the hands of the founder. Their clothing is blue and purple. They are all the work of skillful men. 10. But the **LORD* is the true God**; He is the **Living God** and an **Everlasting King**. The earth will tremble at His wrath and the nations will not be able to abide His indignation. 11. Thus you will say to them, The **gods** that have **not made the heavens and the earth will perish from the earth** and **from under the heavens**. 12. **He** has made the earth by **His** power. **He** has **established the world** by **His** wisdom and has **stretched out** the **heavens** at **His discretion**. 13. When **He** utters **His** voice, there is a multitude of waters in the heavens and He causes the vapors to ascend from the ends of the earth. He makes lightnings with rain and brings forth the wind out of His treasuries. 14. Every man is ignorant in his knowledge, every **refiner** is put to shame by his **graven image**. It is **falsehood** and there is **no breath** in them. 15. They are **vanity**, the work of errors. They will perish in the **time of their visitation (punishment)**. 16. The **Portion of Jacob** is not like them, for He is the **Creator** of all things and **Israel** is the rod of His inheritance: **The LORD* of Hosts is His name**.*

In verse seven, **King of Nations** could also be translated as **King of the Heathens**. In verse eight, **Vanities** refers to **worthless**, **vain** things – the products of **man's thoughts**. Those who put stock in those worthless things are not aware when the time comes for **Judgment**. They do not know God and do not have a relationship with the **LORD* of Hosts**. In verse sixteen, **Portion of Jacob** relates to Psalm 16:5 and Jeremiah 51:19, which say the **LORD*** is my **Portion**.

*Jeremiah 11:22. Therefore thus says the **LORD* of Hosts**, Behold, I shall **punish** them. The young men will die by the **sword**, their sons and their daughters will die by **famine**, 23. and there will be no remnant of them, for I shall bring evil upon the men of Anatoth, the **year of their visitation**.*

Jeremiah 48:42. *And **Moab** will be **destroyed** from being a **people**, because it has magnified (itself) against the **LORD****. 43. Terror and the pit and the snare will be upon you, O inhabitant of **Moab**, says the **LORD****. 44. He who flees from fear will fall into the pit; and he who gets up out of the pit will be taken in the snare, for I shall bring upon it, upon **Moab**, the year of their **visitation** (**punishment**), says the **LORD****.*

1 Peter 2:11. *Beloved, I urge (you) as strangers and sojourners to abstain from (the) desires of the flesh that are warring against your very beings: 12. so have your good way of life among the heathens, (as a living example to them), so that, while they will speak evil of you as of evildoers, when they observe your **good deeds** (then) they would glorify God on (the) **Day of visitation**.*

The **Good Deeds** are the **acts of Loving Kindness** of believers. The **Day of Visitation** is **Judgment Day,** the separation of the **Sheep** from the **Goats**. **Acts of Loving Kindness** are whatever **Acts** are done by Saints that exceed God's minimum Standard of Righteousness.

Matthew 25:41. *"Then He will also say to those on His **left**, 'You, the ones who have been **cursed**, must continually go from Me into the **eternal fire** prepared for the **devil** and **his angels**. 42. For **I** was **hungry** and you did **not** give Me anything to eat, I was **thirsty** and you did **not** give Me a drink, 43. **I** was a **stranger** and you did **not** take Me in, **poorly clothed** and you did **not** clothe Me, **sick** and in **prison** and you did **not** visit **Me.**' 44. Then they also answered saying to Him, '**Lord**, when did we see **You hungry** or **thirsty** or a **stranger** or **poorly clothed** or **sick** or in **jail** and we did **not** serve You?' 45. Then He will answer them saying, 'Truly I say to you, in so much as you did **not** do something for **one of the least of these**, you did **not** do it for **Me.**' 46. And **they will go into eternal punishment**, but the **righteous into eternal life.**"*

The reference to **Eternal Punishment** is clearly to **Judgment Day**. God requires each one of us to **Love My neighbor as Myself!**

Time of their Visitation is an expression for **Judgment Day!** That **Day** is **not** a **twenty-four-hour day** like we now have, but is extended over a **very**

long time since the Sun and the Moon are destroyed toward the end of the **Day**. There is **no** time in the **Spirit Realm**.

> Jude 5. *And I wish to remind you, that you all know that the **Lord** has saved people, once for all from the land of Egypt, but the **second** (time) He **destroyed** those who did **not** believe, (Numbers 14:28,29) 6. and those **angels** who did **not** keep themselves (from the) beginning, but who **deserted their own dwelling places**, He has kept (those angels) in **eternal chains** in darkness (2 Pet. 2:4) for **judgment** on (the) great **Day**. 7. Again, take **Sodom** and **Gomorrah** and the **cities around them**, which indulged in **immorality** and went after other **flesh**, (in **immorality**), as they (continue to) undergo (the) **punishment of eternal fire** they are exhibited as a horrible example, (a warning to others).*

The **Angels** who deserted their own **dwelling places** willfully left their **sanctuaries**, their own **sanctified** bodies when they followed **Satan**. On the **Great Day**, **Judgment Day**, they will be sent to the **Lake of Fire**, the **Second Death**.

3

WHAT WE WILL NOT HAVE IN HEAVEN

FROM **COVETOUSNESS** TO **CONTENTMENT**

Life on earth is loaded with **Covetousness**; people want things that others have, from cars, houses, jewelry, fancy clothes, money, spouses, and any other thing someone else has. This also extends into the corporate world and even to the Church, where one pastor does things to increase weekly Sunday attendance in competition with another pastor or any other way his congregation can outdo another church. In Heaven, there will be no sin, no covetousness, no jealousy, no want of any kind. Everyone will be **content** with whatever state he or she is in.

There are many things to which we are accustomed on Earth that will not be in Heaven, including negative emotions.

We will rejoice over negative things that will not be present in the Hereafter:

> Proverb 6:16. *The* **LORD*** *hates these six things, and* **seven** *are an* **abomination to Him***: 17. a* **proud** *look, a* **lying** *tongue, hands that* **shed innocent blood***, 18. a* **heart** *that devises* **wicked imaginations, feet** *that are* **swift in running to evil***, 19. a* **false witness** *who speaks lies, and the* **one who sows discord among brothers***.*

Number One on **God's** list of things **He** Hates is **Pride**; all the occupants of Heaven will be **Humble**, **Repentant**, adding greatly to the wonderful, very pleasant atmosphere there.

Psalm 10:2. *The **wicked** in his **pride** persecutes the poor: they will be taken in the devices that they have imagined. 3. For the wicked **boasts** of his heart's **desire** and the **covetous blesses himself** and **despises** the **LORD***.*

Matthew 6:25. *"Because of this I say to you, **stop being anxious** for your life, what you would **eat** or what you would **drink**, or what you would **put on your body**. No indeed! Is **life** not more than **food** and the **body** (more than) **clothing**? 26. You must consider the birds of the sky that do not sow and do not harvest and do not gather into a storehouse, and your heavenly **Father** feeds them: are you not worth more than they? 27. And who of you if you are **anxious** is able to add one single hour upon his age? 28. And concerning **clothing**, why are you **anxious**? You must observe the **lilies** of the field, how they grow: they do not labor and they do not spin: 29. but I say to you that Solomon in all his glory did **not dress himself as one of these**. 30. And if **God** clothes the grass of the field this way, (which) is (here) today and tomorrow is cast into a furnace, (will He) not much more (clothe) you, little faiths? 31. Therefore you should **not be anxious** saying, 'What could we eat?' or, 'What could we drink?' or, 'What should we wear?' 32. For the heathens are striving for all these things: for indeed your heavenly **Father** knows that you need all these things. 33. But **you must continually seek first the Kingdom of God and His righteousness**, then all these things will be provided for you. 34. Therefore **do not be anxious** for tomorrow, for tomorrow will be **anxious** of itself: (each day's) trouble (is) enough for that day."*

All **anxiety** is banished from the Heavenly Kingdom! **Anxiety** is a curse! In Heaven, our nourishment will not come from **food** but from the **Word of God**! **Clothes will be Spiritual**, with a **White Robe of Righteousness** for each one of us. Other clothing will be worn as a situation demands, as I saw in a heavenly vision when I prayed for a daughter who had been miscarried in 1962; in 1991, in a vision, I saw her wearing a fresh spring frock. To be **Anxious** is a curse, so no one will ever be **Anxious** in Heaven! Things that people are **Anxious** over on earth do not exist in the Hereafter! So, whether you now fret over various possessions or your positions now, those things do not exist in the Spirit Realm! You will be occupied with Praising and Worshipping God Himself and will no longer think of earthly things!

No Works of the Flesh Will be in Heaven!

> Galatians 5:19. *And the **works of the flesh** are apparent, which are **immorality, impurity, licentiousness**, 20. **idolatry, sorcery, enmity, strife, jealousy, anger, outbreaks of selfishness, dissensions, factions**, 21. **envy, drunkenness, carousing**, and like things. I tell you beforehand, just as I told you before, that the ones who are doing things such as these **will not inherit (the) Kingdom of God**.*

It will be wonderful to live without anything on that list! The Greek word translated sorcery is pharmakeia, referring to taking drugs to cause visions or messages from spirits. The word translated drunkenness, methai, refers to any intoxication, including all recreational drugs.

> Ephesians 5:3. *But any **immorality** or **impurity** or **covetousness** must not be named among you, as is fitting for saints, 4. nor **foul speaking** or **foolish talking** or **low jesting**, which things do not belong, but rather thanksgiving. 5. For you know this very well, that **anyone who practices immorality** or **uncleanness** or **covetousness**, who is an **idol-worshipper**, does **not** have any inheritance in the **Kingdom of the Messiah and God**.*

The phrase "idol-worshipper" refers specifically to **covetousness**, so lusting after material things will not exist in Heaven.

> Colossians 3:5. *Therefore you must right now put to **death** the **earthly parts**, (which are) **immorality, uncleanness, passion, evil desires**, and **covetousness**, which is **idol-worship**, 6. because of **which** the wrath of God is coming upon the sons of the disobedient. 7. Among whom you also once walked, when you were living in these things: 8. but now then **you must immediately put everything off from yourself, anger, passion, wickedness, depravity, malice, blasphemy, slander, evil, obscene, abusive speech** from your mouth: 9. you must **not** ever **lie** to one another, since you stripped off the old man with his deeds 10. and by putting on your new (self), which is being renewed in knowledge according to (the) image of the **One** Who **created** (the **universe**), 11. where (there is) not one **Greek** or **Jewish, circumcision** or **uncircumcision**, barbarian, Scythian, slave, free, but then **Messiah** (is) **all things** to all those.*

28

Idol-Worshipper again refers specifically to **Covetousness**, while **Which** refers to the entire list in verse 5. **Slander** is often **Gossip** and is one of the most common sins.

> Mark 7:20. *And He was saying, "That going out from a person defiles him. 21. For the **evil purposes within** go out from the **hearts** of people, **immoralities, stealing, murder**, 22. **adultery, covetousness, deceit, sensuality, stinginess, blasphemy, pride, foolishness:** 23. **all these evils within** go out and **defile the person**."*

In verse 20, **Y'shua** is saying that we do **not** lose eternal life by what we eat, but we do know that our life on Earth is shortened by what we eat, ignoring Acts 15:20 *to **abstain** from the **pollutions** of the **idols** and from **immorality** and from the (meat) of (**strangled**) **animals** and from the **blood**.* All meat had to be killed according to the regulations, describing the proper methods for killing the sacrificial animal so the animal being offered would not suffer and would maximize drainage of blood. People suffer by ignoring Tanach's warnings and by overeating. In verse twenty-one, **Immoralities** consist of **all forms of idolatry**, including heresy. **Stinginess** in verse twenty-two is literally '**evil eye**,' which is a Hebrew idiom for being **greedy** or **stingy**.

Relief for the Repentant

> Isaiah 57:14. *And He will say, Lift up! Lift up! Prepare the way! Take up the **stumbling block** out of the way of **My** people! 15. For thus says the **High** and **Lofty One** Who inhabits eternity, Whose name is **Holy**, I dwell in the high and holy place, with him who is also of a remorseful and **humble** spirit, to revive the spirit of the **humble**, and to revive the heart of the **repentant** ones. 16. For I shall not contend forever, neither will I always be angry, for the spirit should fail before Me, and the souls which I have made. 17. For the **iniquity of his covetousness** I was **angry** and **struck him**. I **hid Myself** and was **angry** and he went on sinfully in the way of his heart. 18. I have seen his ways and will heal him. I shall lead him also and restore comforts to him and to his mourners. 19. I create the speech of the lips. **Peace**. **Peace** to him that is far off and to him that is near! says the **LORD***, and I shall heal him. 20. But the **wicked** are like the troubled sea, when it cannot rest,*

*whose waters cast up mire and dirt. 21. There is **no shalom**, says my **God**, for the **wicked**.*

The **Stumbling Blocks** are evil thoughts, leading astray those who would **Repent**. Their guilty conscience leads to the curse of **anxiety**, away from **Peace**.

Jeremiah 6:13. *For from the least of them even to the greatest of them everyone is given to **covetousness**, and from the **prophet** even to the **priest** everyone deals falsely. 14. They have also healed the hurt of My people lightly saying, **Peace. Peace!** when there is **no peace**. (1 Thessalonians 5:3) 15. Were they ashamed when they had committed abominations? No, they were not at all ashamed, neither could they blush. Therefore they will fall among those who fall, at the time I **visit** them they will be cast down, says the LORD*.*

Covetousness is very broad, far beyond the common jealousy concerning possessions. The **LORD*** will **Visit, Punish** the sinners near the end and at the end of Judgment Day.

Proverb 28:16. *The prince who wants understanding is also a great oppressor. He that **hates covetousness** will prolong (his) days.*

We do know that this statement is true, that the person will enter **ETERNAL LIFE**, being **Content, while** prolonging his or her days forever.

Luke 12:13. *And someone from the crowd said to Him, "Teacher, **You must now tell my brother** to divide the **inheritance** with me." 14. But He said to him, "Sir, who appointed Me a judge or arbitrator over you?" 15. And He said to them, "You must continually understand and **guard yourselves from all covetousness**, because someone's life is **not abundant from his possessions**."*

It is **Covetousness** that makes the questioner ask for his portion of the inheritance; not a good sign! That someone's life is **not** abundant because of **possessions** shows that the **prosperity teachings** are not appropriate. We are to focus on God, **not** on money or other possessions.

Exodus 20:14. *"You will **not <u>covet</u> your neighbor's house, you will not <u>covet</u> your neighbor's wife**, or **his manservant**, or **his maidservant**, or **his ox**, or **his donkey**, or **anything that is your neighbor's.**"*

Covetousness is a really significant **Sin,** so be careful you do not fall into that trap while you are on earth. This is a trap that will **not** exist in Heaven because only the **Humble** will be there! There will be **no** possessions to tempt us, **no** jewelry to show off, **no** mansions to tempt others to covet yours! Everything in Heaven will be **Spirit!** The flowers will be **Spirit**; those who walk on the flowers will be **Spirit,** so the flowers will not be tamped down underfoot but will go through the feet of those who walk on them. We will not eat but will feed and grow on the **Word of God!**

Matthew 7.1. *"**Do not judge**, so that you would not **be judged**: 2. for in which judgment you **judge**, you will **be judged**, and in the **measure** in which you **measure**, it will be **measured** to you. (Rom. 14:10-13)*

No one will judge you in Heaven because the **Great White Throne Judgment** has approved your promotion to the **Spirit Realm.**

Luke 6:37. *"And (if you) **do not judge**, then you would **not be judged**: and (if you) do **not** condemn, then you would **not** be condemned. You must set free, then you will be set free: 38. you must give, then it will be given to you: they will give a good **measure, pressed down, shaken, poured into your bosom**: for, in which **measure** you **measure**, it will be **measured** to you in return."*

The passage in Luke is given at a different place and time but in the same theme as that in Matthew.

Matthew 7:3. *Then why are you looking at the **speck** in your brother's eye, but you do **not** perceive the **beam** in **your eye**? 4. Or how will you say to your brother, 'You must let me cast the **speck** from your eye,' and there is this **beam** in your eye? 5. Hypocrite! First you must cast the **beam** from your eye, and then you will see clearly to cast out the **speck** from your brother's eye. 6. Do not give the **sacred** things to* *the **dogs** and do not cast your **pearls** before the **swine**, lest they will trample them with their feet, then when they turn they will tear you (to pieces)."*

No one in Heaven will **Judge** anyone else, so you will never **Judge another Spirit, nor will you ever be Judged** after the end of **Judgment Day**! There will be no **healings** in **Heaven** because there is **no sickness** there, neither is there any **physical crippling** or **deformity**; each **Spirit body is perfect!** There will be no **blind**, **deaf**, or **mute**. There will be **no temptation.**

Proverb 2:10. *When **wisdom** comes into your heart and **knowledge** is pleasant to your soul: 11. discretion will preserve you, understanding will keep you, 12. **to deliver you from the way of the bad person,** from the one who **speaks deceitful** things; 13. who leaves the paths of uprightness to walk in the ways of darkness; 14. who enthusiastically **rejoices to do bad things, delighting in the deceitfulness of the wicked;** 15. whose ways are crooked, and who are deceiving in their paths, 16. to deliver you from the **strange woman**, from the **stranger** who flatters with her words, 17. who **forsakes** the **friend of her youth** and forgets the **covenant** of her God.*

The **Strange Woman** represents two things, the **Harlot** and **Heresy**. The **Harlot** represents all **Immorality** and **Covetousness. Heresy** represents **distortion of Scripture, idol worship**, and **false doctrines**, like the prosperity message.

Proverb 2:18. *For her house inclines to **death** and her paths to the dead. 19. No one who goes to her **returns** again, neither do they reach the **paths of life**. 20. So you can walk in the **Way** of **good** people and keep the **paths** of the **righteous**. 21. For the upright will dwell in the land and the man of integrity will remain in it. 22. But the **wicked** will be **cut off** from the earth and the **treacherous** will be **rooted out** of it.*

Death is ETERNAL DEATH in the Lake of Fire, No one **Returns**, repenting, but never reaches the path of **Life**, meaning ETERNAL LIIFE. That is the **Way** of **Good people**. The **treacherous,** who are Sinners, will be **Rooted Out!**

Proverb 3.1. *My son,* **Do not forget my teaching!** *Let your heart keep my commandments, 2. for they will add length of days and* **years of life** *and* **peace** *to you.*

Solomon says his teachings will lead you to years of life, **ETERNAL LIFE!**

Proverb 3:6. *In all your* **Ways know Him** *and* **He** *will make your paths smooth!*

Keep the **Way** of the LORD*, because **Knowing Him** and staying in the **Way** leads unerringly to **ETERNAL LIFE.**

Strife and Contention do **not exist in Heaven.**

Genesis 13:5. *And* **Lot also**, *who went with* **Abram**, *had flocks, herds, and tents. 6. And the land was* **not** *able to bear them, so they could dwell together, for their possessions were great, so that they could not dwell together. 7. And there was* **strife** *between the herdsmen of* **Abram's** *cattle and the herdsmen of* **Lot's** *cattle. And the Canaanites and the Perizzites then dwelled in the land.*

The phrase, "**Lot also**" in verse five indicates that **Lot** was **not among the disciples**. He was there because he was family. The **Strife** is evidence of Lot's **Not** being saved.

Genesis 13:8. *And* **Abram** *said to* **Lot**, *"****There must be <u>no</u> strife***, *I pray you, between me and you, and between my herdsmen and your herdsmen, for* **we are brothers**. *9. Is not the whole land before you? Separate yourself from me, I pray you, if you will take the left hand, then I shall go to the right, or if you go to the right hand, then I shall go to the left."*

Kinship meant a great deal from the very beginning of mankind on earth and will continue to be meaningful in the hereafter when we go to be with our fathers.

Genesis 13:10. *And* **Lot** *lifted up his eyes, and looked at the whole plain of Jordan, that it was well watered everywhere before the LORD* *destroyed Sodom and Gomorrah, even like the garden of the LORD*, *like the land of Egypt, as you come to Zoar. 11. Then **Lot** chose for himself all the plain of the Jordan and **Lot** journeyed east, and they separated themselves the one from the other.*

Lot selfishly chose the best for himself. There will be **No selfishness** in **Heaven.**

Violence will not exist in Heaven

Genesis 21:22. *And it happened at that time that **Abimelech and Fikhol the chief captain of his army** spoke to **Abraham** saying, "God is with you in all that you do. 23. Now therefore swear to me here by God that you will not deal falsely with me or with my son, or with my son's son, but according to the loving kindness that I have done for you, you will do to me, and to the land in which you have sojourned." 24. And Abraham said, "I shall swear." 25. And **Abraham reproved Abimelech** because of a **well of water**, which **Abimelech's servants had <u>violently</u> taken away**. 26. And Abimelech said, "I do not know who has done this thing: neither did you tell me, but I heard of it just today." 27. And **Abraham** took sheep and oxen, and gave them to **Abimelech**, and both of them **cut a covenant**. 28. And **Abraham** set seven ewe-lambs of the flock by themselves. 29. And **Abimelech** said to **Abraham**, "What do these seven ewe-lambs mean that you have set by themselves?" 30. And he said, "For you will take these seven ewe-lambs from my hand, so they may be a **witness** to me, that **I have dug this well**." 31. Therefore he called that place Beer-Sheba because both of them swore there.*

There will be **no** disputes in Heaven, **no** arguments, **no** claims, **no** ownership, **no** covetousness; there will be **no** feeling of "I know my rights!" The Hebrew verb Sheva means To swear an oath, and the adjective Sheva means seven.

Beer-Sheba is translated in two different ways: The Hebrew verb Sheva means To swear an oath, and the adjective Sheva means Seven. Be'er means Well, so, Well of Oath or Well of Seven; both are correct. The latter is a reference to the seven ewes of verse twenty-eight. The word "Beer-Sheba" has the letter "B" instead of "V" because that was translated from Latin or

Greek and not from Hebrew. Latin and Greek have **No** letter "V," so they use "B" instead of "V."

No Killing for political or any other reason.

> Matthew 2:13. *And after they went away, behold, an **angel** of the Lord revealed to Joseph in a dream saying, "**When you get up, you must immediately take the child and His mother** and **flee into Egypt** and you must be there until whenever I tell you: for Herod is going to seek the child to **kill Him**." 14. Then after he got up he took the child and His mother in the night and he went away into Egypt, 15. and he was there until the **death of Herod**: so that the word of the Lord by the prophet would be fulfilled saying, "I called My Son out of Egypt."* (Hos. 11.1)

God orders Joseph to take the mother and Y'shua down to Egypt because Herod would try to kill Y'shua; this happened about two years after the birth of Y'shua. When the family was no longer living in the cave where **Y'shua** was born, they were instead living in a house.

> Matthew 2:7. *Then Herod, having secretly called the astrologers, ascertained from them the time of the revealing of (the) star, 8. and sending them into Bethlehem he said, "When you go you must inquire carefully concerning the child: as soon as you would find (**Him**), you must report to me right away, then when I come I shall pay homage to **Him**." 9. And those who heard the king went. And lo! The star, which they saw in the east, led them forth, until it came (and) stood over where the child was. 10. And when they saw the star they rejoiced (with) extremely great joy. 11. Then when they came into the **house** they saw the **child with Miriam His mother**, and having fallen (to their knees) they paid homage to Him, then, having opened their **treasure boxes**, they brought gifts to Him, **gold** and **frankincense** and **myrrh**. 12. And since they had been warned in a dream **not** to return to Herod, they returned to their country by another way.*

That **Y'shua**, **Miriam**, and **Joseph** were in a **house**, not the cave/barn where **Y'shua** was born, shows that considerable time had elapsed after **His** birth.

The Slaying of the Infants

Matthew 2:16. *Then after Herod saw that he was tricked by the astrologers he became exceedingly angry, and he sent and **killed** all the male children in Bethlehem and in all the regions of it from **two years old and below**, according to the time which he ascertained from the astrologers. 17. Then that spoken by Jeremiah the prophet was fulfilled saying,*
18. *"A voice was heard in Rama,*
weeping and" much "mourning:
Rachel weeping for her children,
*and she was not to be comforted, because **they were not**."* (Jer. 31:14)

"They were not" is a Hebrew idiom meaning they were dead.

Matthew 12:14. *After the **Pharisees** left they formed a plan against Him, how they could **kill** Him (**Y'shua**).*

Matthew 14.1. *In that time **Herod the Tetrarch** heard of the **fame** of **Y'shua**, 2. and he said to his servants, "This is **John the Immerser**: he rose from the dead and because of this the miracles are operating in him." 3. For after **Herod** arrested **John** he bound him and put him away in prison because (**Herod's** wife) Herodiah (had been)) the wife of **Philip** his brother: 4. for **John** was saying to him, "It is not permitted for you to have her." 5. And while he wanted to **kill him** he was afraid of the crowd, because they held him as a **prophet**. 6. And when it was a birthday celebration of **Herod**, the daughter of **Herodiah** danced in their midst and pleased **Herod**, 7. then with an oath he promised to give her whatever she would ask. 8. And she, urged by her mother, said, "**You must immediately give me the head of John the Immerser** here upon a plate." 9. Then although the king was saddened, because of the oaths and those who were reclining together with him, he commanded it to be given, 10. so then he sent (and) **beheaded John** in the prison. 11. And his head was brought on a platter and was given to the girl, and she brought (it) to her mother. 12. Then after his disciples came they took the body and they buried it and when they came to **Y'shua** they reported (what happened).*

John the Immerser was another political prisoner killed for his preaching.

There will be No stealing in Heaven.

Luke 16.1. *And then He was saying to the disciples, "A certain man was wealthy, who had a manager, and this (owner) brought charges against him because he was squandering (the owner's) wealth. 2. Then when he called him he said to him, 'What is this I hear about you? You must immediately give back the title of your office, for you are not able to still manage.' 3. But the manager said to himself, 'What will I do, because my employer is taking away the office from me? I am not strong enough to dig, I am ashamed to beg. 4. I know what I shall do, so that when I would be deposed from the office they will take me into their homes.' 5. Then after he summoned each one of his employer's debtors he said to the first,* **'How much do you owe my employer?'** *6. And he said,* **'A hundred baths of olive oil.'** *and he said to him, 'You must take your notes and after you sit down, you must quickly write* **fifty (baths).'** *7. Then to another he said,* **'And how much do you owe?'** *And he said,* **'A hundred cors of wheat.'** *He said to him, 'You must take your documents and you must now write* **eighty.'** *8. Then the employer praised the unjust manager; that he did wisely: because* **the sons of this age are wiser than the sons of the light in their own generation**.

A hundred baths of olive oil is 800-900 gallons, an awesome amount; fifty baths are worth half that. A hundred cors of wheat is about 1,000 bushels, another awesome sum. Then **Y'shua** sums up the situation by saying the sons of this age are wiser than the sons than the **Sons of Light**, showing that our focus is to be on **Kingdom**, not **Money**. There will be **no** dishonesty in Heaven, **no** wealth, **no** money, **no** things, **no** possessions, and **no** one to tempt another person.

The Rich Man and Lazarus

Luke 16:19. *"And there was a certain* **wealthy** *man, and he dressed in a* **purple garment** *and* **fine linen**, **enjoying himself splendidly day after day**. *20. And some poor (man) named* **Lazarus**, *covered with sores, had been lying at his gate 21.* **desiring to be fed from the things that fell from the table** *of the* **wealthy** *one: but even the dogs that came were licking his sores. 22. And it happened the* **poor man** *died and was carried away by the angels to the **bosom of Abraham**: and then the rich man died and was buried. 23. And in **Hades**, as he was in **torment**, when he lifted up his eyes he saw **Abraham** from afar and **Lazarus** in front of him. 24. Then when he called out he said, 'Father **Abraham**, you must immediately have mercy on me and you must now send **Lazarus** so that he could dip the tip of his finger in water and it would cool my tongue, because **I am suffering in this flame.**' 25. But **Abraham** said, 'Child, you must remember that **you took your good things in your life**, and **Lazarus likewise the bad things**: but now here he is **comforted**, and you are in **great pain**. 26. And in all these (distances) between us and you, a great **chasm** has been established, so that those **who wish to cross over from here to you would not be able**, and they **could not cross from there to us**.' 27. And he said, 'Then I ask you, Father, that you would send **him** to my **father's** house, 28. for I have five brothers, so that he could warn them, so that they would not come into this place of torture.' 29. But **Abraham** said, '**They have Moses and the Prophets**: they must **listen to them now**.' 30. But he said, 'No, Father **Abraham**, but if someone from (the) **dead** would go to them they will repent.' 31. But he said to him, 'If they do not listen to **Moses and the Prophets, then they will not be persuaded if someone would rise from (the) dead.**'"*

The **Bosom of Abraham** is an idiom referring to the **place of honor at a banquet**, although here, it refers to his being **next to Abraham**, a partaker of the same blessedness as **Abraham** in Paradise. **Earthly Wealth** does not transfer into **Heaven**, where there is **no** wealth, **no** stocks, **no** bonds, **no** Mutual funds, **no** Title Deeds, and **no** possessions of any kind. Those who have handled their money in a Godly way on Earth will receive a reward, but the reward will be measured in **God's Love**; it will **not** be measured in currency or gold, or any physical thing we value.

The Parable of the Ten Minas

Luke 19:11. *And while they were listening to these things He again told them a parable because He was near Jerusalem and they thought that the **Kingdom of God** was going to be revealed at once, (as soon as He reached Jerusalem). 12. Therefore He said, "A certain man, a* *nobleman, was going to a far away land to take a **kingdom for himself**, then to **return**. 13. And after he called his ten **servants** he gave **ten minas** to them and said to them, 'You must **do business** while I am gone.' 14. But its **citizens hated him** and they sent ambassadors after him saying, '**We do not want this one to reign** over us.' 15. Then it happened when **he returned**, after he took the **kingdom**, that he said to summon to him those **servants** to whom he had given the money, so that he might know what **they had earned**. 16. And the **first one** appeared saying, 'Lord, **your mina earned ten minas**.' 17. Then he said to **him**, '**Well done! Good servant**, because you were **faithful** in (the) least, you must continually have authority over **ten cities**.' 18. Then the second came saying, '**Your mina, lord, made five minas**.' 19. And he said to this one also, 'Then you must continually be over **five cities**.' 20. Then the other one came saying, 'Lord, behold **your mina**, which I have put away in a **handkerchief**. 21. for I was **fearing you**, because you are a **severe man**, you take what you did not put away and you harvest what you did not sow.' 22. He said to him, 'From your **mouth I judge you, evil servant**. Had you known that I am a **severe man**, taking out what I did not put in and reaping what I did not sow? 23. Then why did you not give my money on a changer's table? Then when I came I (would have) exacted with interest.' 24. And to those who were standing by he said, 'You must now take the **mina from him** and you must **give (it) at once to the one who has ten minas**' 25. – then they said to him, 'Lord, he has **ten minas**.' – 26. I say to you that **to everyone who has it will be given**, but from the **one who does not have even what he does have will be taken**. – 27. 'Moreover my **enemies**, those who do not want me to reign over them, you must right now lead (them) here and you must **slaughter them in front of me**.'"*

A mina equals 50 shekels, which is about 100 drachmas or 100 denarii, a few months' wages. This parable is a picture of Ezekiel 9 where the man with the Inkhorn marks the Saints, then he and the other five with him, Strike the Sinners. The Saints know the Word of God, and their actions are evidence of their faith, so the first two Servants put the LORD*'s message, the **minas,** to work in their lives and are rewarded for that when the LORD* returns. Those who did not work with the message are killed in front of the LORD*. That is exactly how it will be on Judgment Day.

The Cleansing of the Temple

Luke 19:45. And when He entered the Temple He began to cast out the sellers, 46. saying to them, "It has been written,
*'And **My house will be a house of prayer**,' (Isa. 56:7)*
but you have made it a robbers' cave." (Jer. 7:11)
*47. And He was teaching daily in the Temple. And the high priests and the scribes and the leaders of the people were seeking to **kill Him**, 48. but they did not find what they could do, because all the people were hanging upon (what) they were hearing from **Him**.*

There are those today who use the pulpit for personal gain, but they are not making points with God. There are ministries today worth many millions of dollars, but that does not bless the LORD*.

The Parable of the Vineyard and the Tenants

Luke 20:9. And He began to tell this parable to the people: "A certain man planted a vineyard, then leased it to farmers and went on a journey for a long time. 10. And in time he sent a servant to the farmers so that they would give him from the fruit of the vineyard: but the farmers, after they beat him, sent (him) out empty-handed. 11. Then he again sent another servant: but after they beat and dishonored that one also, they sent him out empty-handed. 12. And again he sent a third: and after they also wounded this one they threw (him) out. 13. And the master of the vineyard said, 'What will I do? I shall send my beloved son: they will probably respect him.' 14. But when they saw him the farmers were discussing with one another saying, 'This one is the heir: we should kill him, so that the inheritance would be ours.' 15. Then after they threw him outside the vineyard they killed (him). What therefore will the master of the vineyard do to them? 16. He will come and he will destroy these farmers and he will give the vineyard to others." When they heard they said, "May it not be!" 17. And looking at them He said, "Then why has this been written:

'A stone which the builders rejected,
this has become the cornerstone.' (Ps. 118:22)

Each of these parables about the vineyard uses a picture of greedy farmers to speak of the High Priest and other Jewish leaders. The message also applies to a number of present-day Church leaders.

Luke 20:18. *Everyone who falls upon that stone will be dashed to pieces: on whomever it would fall, it will crush him." 19. And the scribes and the high priests sought to get their hands on Him in that hour, for they knew that He spoke against them in this parable, but they feared the people.*

Falsely Accused

Nehemiah 6:4. *Yet they sent to me four times after this sort and I answered them after the same manner. 5. Then Sanballat sent his servant to me in like manner the **fifth time with an open letter** in his hand 6. in which was written, It is reported among the nations and Gashmu (Geshem) says, **You and the Jews are thinking of rebellion**, for which **cause** you are **building the wall**, so you could be their **king**, according to these words. 7. And you have also appointed prophets to preach at Jerusalem saying, **There is a king in Judah** and now **it will be reported to the king** according to these words. Come now therefore and let us take counsel together.*

Nehemiah 6:8. *Then I sent to him saying, **There are no such things done** such as you are saying, but **you feign them out of your own heart**. 9. For they all put us in awe saying, Their hands will be weakened from the work, so it will not be done. Now therefore, strengthen my hands.*

There will be **No Lies, No False Accusations** in Heaven!

Paul Falsely Accused

Acts 21:27. *And since the seven days were completed, as they were going (into the Temple), **Jewish** men from **Asia**, when they saw **him** in the **Temple**, were stirring the whole crowd and they seized **him** 28. crying out, "Men of Israel, you must help: this is the man, the **one who teaches everyone everywhere against our people and the***

*Torah (Teaching) and this place, and what's more he even **led Greeks into the Temple** and **he has profaned this holy place.**" 29. For they had previously seen **Trophimus the Ephesian in the city with him, whom they were supposing that Paul led into the Temple**. 30. And the whole city was aroused, and the people rushed together, then when they took hold of Paul they were dragging him outside the Temple and the doors were immediately shut. 31. And while seeking to kill **him** a report went up to the commander of the cohort that all Jerusalem was in an uproar. 32. He at once took soldiers and a centurion, ran down upon them, and when they saw the commander and the soldiers they stopped beating **Paul**. 33. Then when the commander came near, he arrested **him** and ordered (**him**) to be bound with two chains, (and) then he inquired who he might be and what had been done. 34. But others in the crowd were shouting different things, and since he was not able to know the truth because of the noise he ordered **him** to be led to the barracks. 35. And when they came to the steps, **he** was carried by the soldiers because of the violent pressing of the crowd, 36. for the multitude of the people was following, shouting, "You must take **him** (from among the living)."*

All this was false; lies, because **Paul** taught everywhere to follow Torah, to honor the Seasons of the LORD*. **He** opposed traditions that were not Scriptural but **never** taught **against Torah**. Those lies haunted **Paul** for the rest of **his** life, but now in **Heaven, Paul** has no more **False Accusations** stirring up unrest around **him**.

Bondage, Either Physical or Spiritual, will not exist:

Exodus 1:13. *And the Egyptians made the children of Israel serve with harshness. 14. And they made their lives bitter with hard **bondage**, in mortar, in brick, and in all manner of service in the field: all their service, in which they made them serve, was with harshness.*

Exodus 20.1. *And God spoke **all these words** saying, 2. "**I AM** the LORD* your God Who has brought you out of the land of Egypt, **out of the house of bondage**.*

The LORD* spoke <u>all these words</u>; not just the Ten Statements. In Exodus 20, Forty days were not needed for writing just the Ten Statements, but the LORD* wrote all the instructions on the tablets, Deut. 9:10, front and back. What Moses wrote was placed beside the Ark, Deut. 31:26.

Both Jews and Christians make the mistake of putting emphasis on the Ten Commandments, an emphasis that the LORD* avoided.

The Torah (Teaching) and the Kingdom of God

> Luke 16:14. *The **Pharisees were listening** to all these things and since they were **lovers of money** they were sneering at **Him**. 15. Then **He** said to them, "**You are justifying yourselves before men**, but **God knows your hearts**: because the **one who is exalted among men** (is) an **abomination before God**. 16. The Torah (Teaching) and the Prophets (were proclaimed) until John: from then on the **Kingdom of God** is being preached and **everyone enters it forcibly**. (Matt. 11:12) 17. And it is easier for heaven and Earth to pass away than for one **vav** of the **Torah** (Teaching) to fall. (Matt. 5:18) 18. Everyone who divorces his wife and marries another is committing adultery, and the man who marries (her) when she has been divorced from (her) husband is committing adultery."*

The Pharisees loved money and taught the prosperity message, much like those who teach today's prosperity message.

> Jeremiah 34:12. *Therefore the word of the LORD* came to **Jeremiah** from the LORD* saying, 13. Thus says the LORD*, the God of Israel, **I AM** cut a covenant with your fathers in the day that I brought them forth out of the land of Egypt, out of the **house of bondage** saying, 14. At the **end of seven years** each man let his Hebrew brother go who has been sold to you, and when he has served you **six years**, you will let him **go free from you**, but your fathers did not listen to Me or incline their ear.*

At the end of **six years,** each Hebrew slave is **Free** to go! When that command is not followed under Nehemiah, Nehemiah reinforces the command.

Nehemiah 5:5. *Yet now our flesh is like the flesh of our brothers, our children as their children and see, we bring our sons and our daughters into bondage to be servants, and some of our daughters have already been brought into **bondage**. Neither is it in our power to redeem them, for other men have our lands and vineyards.* (Jer. 34:8ff)

Matthew 7:31. *And again when He came out from the territory of Tyre He came through Sidon to the lake of Galilee through the territories of the **Ten Cities**. 32. And they were bringing a deaf and speech-impaired man to Him and they were begging Him to lay His hand on him. 33. And after He took him privately aside from the crowd, He cast His fingers into his ears, and after He spit He touched his tongue, 34. and then He looked up into the sky, sighed and was saying to him in Hebrew, "**Hippatach**," (Isa. 61:1) that is "You must right now be opened." 35. And immediately his hearing did open and the **bondage** of his tongue was loosed and he was speaking correctly.*

Bondage is the operative word for both slavery and demon-possession.

Ten cities, nine east of the Jordan plus Beit-Sh'an, were declared "**Free Cities**" by Rome. These cities are all south and/or east of the lake, while Tyre and Sidon are northwest of the lake, about fifty miles away. See **Dekapolis** in Glossary. **Hippatach** is the word in the Hebrew Scripture of Isaiah 61:1 "to open the prison.." It refers specifically to opening eyes and ears, both physical and spiritual. Anyone who needed deliverance was in **Bondage**, just as today there are hundreds of millions in both Physical and Spiritual **Bondage,** but in the Spirit Realm, there will be no **Bondage**, either Spiritual **Bondage** or Physical **Bondage.**

Psalm 107:10. *Such as sit in **darkness** and in the **shadow of death**, **bound in affliction and iron**, 11. because they rebelled against the words of God and condemned the counsel of the **Most High**.*

David puts both Spiritual Bondage and Physical Bondage in verse ten. **No** form of **Bondage** will exist in the Hereafter.

Zechariah 8:16. *These are the things that you will do: Everybody speak the truth to his neighbor, execute the judgment of truth and peace in* *your gates, (Eph. 4:25) 17. and **do not any of you devise evil in your hearts against his neighbor**, and **do not love any false oath**, for all these are things that **I hate**, says the **LORD***.*

Zechariah 8:23. *Thus says the LORD* of Hosts, In those days it will be that **ten men** from all the **languages of the nations** will take hold, yes they will take hold of the **wings of the garment of him that is Jewish**, saying, We will go with you, for we have heard that **God is with you**.*

The **Wings** of the garment are the folds of the Prayer Shawl worn by all Jewish men in the first century. Everyone will be **Jewish** in the Hereafter!

Our bodies in Heaven will not be physical, so there will be **No** physical attraction or immorality! There will also be **No aches or pains!**

Mark 7.1. *And **Pharisees** and some of the scribes, having come from Jerusalem, gathered to Him. 2. And having seen some of His disciples, that they were eating meals with **common, that is unwashed, hands** 3. for the Pharisees and all the Jewish people if they cannot wash their hands with (the) fist, (using the clenched fist to scrub the open hand), they do not eat, since they carefully keep the **tradition** of the elders, 4. and (when they come) from a market, unless they could immerse themselves they do not eat, and then there are many other traditions which they accepted to keep, immersing cups and pitchers and kettles and lids – 5. and the Pharisees and the scribes would ask Him, "Why are Your disciples not walking according to the **tradition** of the elders, but they are eating a meal with unwashed hands?" 6. And He said to them, "Isaiah rightly prophesied about you hypocrites, as it has been written that*

'This people honors Me with their lips

but their hearts are far away and distant from Me:

7. In vain are they worshipping Me

when they teach (for) instruction the commandments of men.' (Isa. 29:13)

*8. Having canceled the commandment of God you are holding the **tradition** of men." 9. And He was saying to them, "You are just reject-ing the commandment of God, so that you could establish your **tradi-***

tion. 10. For Moses said, 'Honor your father and your mother,' (Exod. 20:12) and 'The one who speaks evil of father or mother surely dies.' (Exod. 21:17) 11. But you are saying, 'If a man would say to father or mother, "Korban," which is "Gift (to God)," whatever you would have received from me,' 12. And you no longer permit him to do anything for his father or his mother, 13. so you make void the Word of God by your tradition which you had passed on: and you are doing many things such as these."

In the Hereafter, eating the Word of God daily will provide all the nourishment our Spiritual bodies will need; all **Traditions** will be ignored and forgotten.

Mark 10:42. *And after He summoned them Y'shua said to them, "You know that those who are considered to lead the heathens are lording over them and (that) the great ones of them tyrannize them. 43. But it is not so among you, but whoever would wish to become great among you will be your servant, 44. and whoever among you would wish to be first will be servant of all: 45. for also the Son of Man did not come to be served but to serve and to give His life as a ransom in exchange for many."*

Each **Spirit** in Heaven will view himself or herself as a **Humble Servant**. In Heaven there will be no **Pride!**

Psalm 49:13. *Nevertheless man being in honor does not abide: he is like the beasts (that) perish. 14. Their way is their folly, yet their posterity approve their sayings. Selah. 15. They are laid in the grave like sheep. Death will feed them and the upright will have dominion over them in the morning and their form will waste away because of the grave having become their dwelling.*

Those who enjoy fame and fortune on earth will seldom, if ever, enjoy the gift of Heaven.

Psalm 49: 17. *Do not be in awe when one is made rich, when the glory of his house is increased! 18. For when he dies he will carry nothing away: his glory, (wealth), will not descend after him.*

19. Though while he lived he blessed his soul; and men will praise you, when you do well for yourself, 20. he will go to the generation of his fathers, who will never see the light. 21. **Man that is in honor** *and does* **not understand** *is like the beasts (that)* **perish.**

You cannot take **fame** or **fortune** with you! You will **Descend**, but your **Wealth or Fame** will **Not** descend with you!

Psalm 53:2. *The* **fool** *has said in his heart,* **There is no God.** *(Psalm 14:1) They are corrupt and have done abominable injustice, there is no one who does good.*

There will **not** be any **Fools** in Heaven!

Psalm 55:22. *The* **words of his mouth were smoother than butter,** *but* **war was in his heart:** *his words were softer than oil, yet they were drawn swords. 23. Cast your burden upon the LORD* and He will sustain you. He will never allow the righteous to be moved.*

There will be no deceit in Heaven where everyone walks **humbly** in repentance every step of every day.

Galatians 5:16. *But I say, may you walk in (the) Spirit so that you would* **not** *in any way fulfill (any)* **desire of the flesh.** *17. For* **flesh** *turns against the* **spirit,** *and the* **spirit** *against the* **flesh,** *these things are opposed to one another, so that you would not do the things you want (to do). 18. But if you are led by (the)* **Spirit,** *you are* **not** *under (the) law (of the* **flesh).** *19. And the* **works of the flesh are apparent,** *which are* **immorality, impurity, licentiousness,** *20.* **idolatry,** **sorcery, enmity, strife, jealousy, anger, outbreaks of selfishness, dissensions, factions,** *21.* **envy, drunkenness, carousing,** *and* **like things.** *I tell you beforehand, just as I told you before, that the* **ones who are doing things such as these will not inherit (the) Kingdom of God.**

As this book is written, our government promotes **Immorality.** **Sorcery** includes pathogens and the drugs to fight them; even the man-made Covid 19 and the drugs to fight it! **Drunkenness** includes more than alcohol since all **"recreational" drugs** are also included. Praise the LORD*! None of these physical drugs will be found in Heaven!

> Matthew 18.1. *In that hour the disciples came to Y'shua saying, "Who is the* **greatest** *in the* **Kingdom of the Heavens?"** *2. And after He called a child to Himself, He stood him in their midst 3. and He said, "Truly I say to you,* **unless you would change and become like the children,** *you could* **not** *enter the* **Kingdom of the Heavens**.

No one who is prideful will ENTER LIFE! Heaven will have no big egos, no bragging, no pushing to get ahead, but everyone will be **Humble**, looking to help everyone else.

> Numbers 11:10. *Then Moses heard the people weep throughout their families, each man in the entrance of his tent, and the* **anger** *of the LORD* was kindled greatly. Moses also was displeased.*

God's **Anger** was kindled because of the people complaining about not having meat. The LORD* definitely does **not** like murmuring and complaining about our circumstances. We, too, have a right to Righteous Indignation against unjust, selfish complaining. The strongest **Anger**, the **Wrath** of the LORD*, is kindled against the worship of **Strange gods**!

> Exodus 32:7. *And the LORD* said to Moses, "Go! Get yourself down! Your people, whom you brought out of the land of Egypt have corrupted themselves. 8. They have* **turned aside quickly out of the Way** *which I commanded them: they have* **made themselves a molten calf** *and have* **worshipped** *it and have* **sacrificed** *to it and said, '**This is your god, O Israel**, that has brought you up out of the land of Egypt.'" 9. And the* **LORD*** *said to* **Moses**, *"I have seen this people and, behold, it is a stiff-necked people. 10. Now therefore let Me alone so My* **wrath** *can* **wax hot** *against them and so I can consume them, and I shall make a great nation of you* **(Moses)."** *11. And* **Moses** *sought the* **LORD*** *his God and said, "LORD*, why does Your wrath wax hot against Your people, whom You have brought out of the land of Egypt with great power and with a mighty hand? 12. Why should the Egyptians speak and say, He brought them out for evil, to slay them in the mountains and to consume them from the face of the earth? Turn*

*from Your fierce **wrath**! And be **sorry** of this evil against Your people. 13. Remember Abraham, Isaac, and Israel, Your servants, to whom You did swear by Your own self and said to them, I shall multiply your seed as the stars of heaven, and all this land that I have spoken of will I give to your seed, and they will inherit it forever." (Heb. 11:12) 14. Then the LORD* was **sorry** for the evil which He said He would do to His people.*

Amos 5:21. *I **hate**, I **despise** your **feast days** and I will not smell the burning **sacrifices** in your solemn assemblies. 22. Though you offer Me **burnt offerings** and your **meal offering**, I will **not accept them**. Nor will I even glance at the **peace offerings** of your fat beasts.*

Hate is another emotion that we get from God, but notice here He **Hates** religious routines from people who are just going through the motions, not presenting their offerings in **Love**.

Proverb 6:16. *The LORD* **hates** these **six things**, and **seven** are an **abomination** to Him: 17. a **proud look**, a **lying tongue**, **hands that shed innocent blood**, 18. a **heart** that **devises wicked imaginations**, **feet** that are **swift in running to evil**, 19. a **false witness** who speaks lies, and the **one who sows discord among brothers**.*

Any **Hate** we have must be related to the **Hate** that God has. Many a church split could have been prevented by observing that last one, sowing **Discord** among the brothers.

Genesis 6:5. *And God saw that the wickedness of man was great in the earth, and every imagination of the thoughts of his heart was continually only bad. 6. And the LORD* was **sorry** that He had made man on the earth, and it **grieved Him** in His heart.*

Ephesians 4:30. *And you must not **grieve** the **Holy Spirit of God**, with Whom you became sealed for the Day of redemption.*

Our Heavenly Father **Grieves!** But there will be no cause for **Grief** in Heaven because There is no **Death** or any serious injury to our **Spirit Bodies**.

PSALM 79

This Psalm is prophetic, along with Psalms 74 and 137, lamenting the coming destruction of the Temple by the Babylonians.

1. A psalm of Asaf. O God, the nations (heathens) have come into Your inheritance. They have defiled Your holy Temple, they have laid Jerusalem on heaps. (Rev. 11:2)

2. They have given the dead bodies of Your servants to be food for the fowls of the sky, the flesh of Your holy ones for the beasts of the earth.

3. They have shed their blood like water around Jerusalem and there was no one to bury them. (Rev. 16:6)

4. We have become a reproach to our neighbors, a scorn and derision to those who are around us.

5. How long, LORD*? Will You be angry forever? How long will Your jealousy burn like fire?

6. Pour out Your wrath upon the nations that have not known, upon the kingdoms that have not called upon Your name.

7. For they have devoured Jacob and laid waste His dwelling place.

8. O do not remember former iniquities against us! Your compassions will speedily prevent us, for we are brought very low.

9. Help us, O God of Our Salvation, for the glory of Your name. Deliver us! Forgive our sins, for Your name's sake.

10. Why should the nations (heathens) say, Where is their God? He will be known among the nations in our sight by the avenging of the shed blood of your servants. (Rev. 6:10; 18:2)

79:11. Let the sighing of the prisoner come before You. According to the greatness of Your power preserve those who are appointed to die, 12. and render sevenfold their reproach to our neighbors into their bosom, with which they have reproached You, my Lord.

13. So we Your people and the sheep of Your pasture will give You thanks forever. We will tell of Your praise to all generations.

Job 1:6. *Now there was a day when the* **children** *of God came to present themselves before the* **LORD****, and* **Satan** *also came among them.*

The **children** of God are all those who **worship Him**, coming on **Rosh HaShannah**, beginning the **Ten Days of Awe** with **repentance**. **Satan** was there to **accuse** each one.

> Job 1:7. *And the **LORD*** said to **Satan**, From where have you come? Then **Satan** answered the **LORD*** and said, From going to and fro on the earth and from walking up and down on it. 8. And the **LORD*** said to **Satan**, Have you considered **My servant Job**, that there is no one like him on the earth, a perfect and an upright man, one who reveres God and turns away from bad?*

The **LORD*** brings up **Job's** name, introducing **Job** into this passage – something Job came to regret in this parable.

> Job 1:9. *Then **Satan** answered the **LORD*** and said, Does **Job** revere **God** for no reason? 10. Have You not made a hedge about him and about his house, and about all that he has on every side? You have **blessed** the work of his hands and his substance is increased in the land, 11. but put out Your hand now and touch all that he has and **he** will **curse You** to Your face. (Rev. 12:10) 12. And the **LORD*** said to **Satan**, Behold, all that he has is in your power, only **do not put forth your hand upon him himself.** So **Satan** went forth from the presence of the LORD*. 13. And there was a day when his sons and his daughters were eating and drinking wine in their oldest brother's house 14. and a messenger came to Job and said, The oxen were plowing and the donkeys feeding beside them 15. and the **Sabeans** fell upon them and took them away. Yea, they have **slain** the **servants** with the edge of the sword and only I have escaped alone to tell you. 16. While he was still speaking, there came also another and said, The **fire of God** has fallen from heaven and has **burned** up the **sheep** and the **servants** and consumed them and only I have escaped to tell you. 17. While he was still speaking, another also came and said, The **Chaldeans** made out three divisions and fell upon the **camels** and have carried them away, yea, and **slain** the **servants** with the edge of the sword and only I have escaped to tell you. 18. While he was still speaking, another also came and said, Your sons and your daughters were eating and drinking wine in their oldest brother's house 19. and, behold, there came a great wind from the wilderness and **smote** the four corners of the **house** and*

*it fell upon the young people and they are **dead** and only I have escaped to tell you. 20. Then **Job** rose and tore his cloak and shaved his head and fell down upon the ground and **worshipped**, 21. and said, Naked I came out of my mother's womb and naked will I return there. The LORD* gave and the LORD* has taken away. **Blessed be the name of the LORD***. 22. With all this **Job** did **not** sin or lay folly to God.*

Satan will have been lost in the **Second Death** by the time all the **Saints** are in **Heaven**, so none of those things can be done, **nor** can any of the **physical atrocities Satan** did to **Job's** body.

Job 4:14:12. *Now a thing was secretly brought to me and my ear took a little of it. 13. In thoughts from the vision of the night, when deep sleep falls on men. 14. **Fear** and **trembling** came upon me, which made all my bones to shake. 15. **Then a spirit passed before my face, the hair of my flesh standing up.***

There will be **No** Fear and **No** Trembling in Heaven!

People will be like Angels!

Matthew 22:23. *In that day **Sadducees**, (who) said there was **no resurrection**, came to **Him** and they asked **Him** 24. saying, "Teacher, **Moses** said, 'If someone would **die** not having children, his **brother** will **marry his wife** and he will **raise** his brother's seed.' (Deut. 25:5) 25. And there were beside us **seven** brothers: and the first married one died, and since he did not have an **heir** he left his **wife** to his **brother**: 26. then likewise the **second** and the **third** until the **seventh**. 27. And **last** of all the **wife** died. 28. Therefore in the resurrection of the seven, whose **wife** will she be? For they all had her." 29. Then **Y'shua** said to them, "You are **misled**, since you do not know either the **Scriptures** or the **power of God**: 30. for in the **resurrection they neither marry nor are given in marriage**, but they will be **like angels in heaven**. 31. And concerning the **resurrection** of the **dead** did you not read what was spoken to you by God saying, 32. '**I AM the God of Abraham and the God of Isaac and the God of Jacob?**' (Exod. 3:6) He is not (the) **God** of the **dead** but (the) **living**." 33. And when the crowds heard (that) they were amazed by His teaching.*

In verse thirty-two, **I AM** is Anochi, the **One** Who can do anything, for **Whom** nothing is impossible or too difficult. The **Resurrected** are alive, but **not physical**.

> Luke 20:27. *And some of the **Sadducees** came, those who were saying there was **not** to be a **resurrection**. They asked **Him** 28. saying, "Teacher, **Moses** wrote for us, if some brother would die, if he had a wife, and this one would be **childless**, that his **brother** would take the **wife** and he would **raise** up a seed for his brother. 29. Then there were seven **brothers**: and the **first**, after he took a wife, died **childless**: 30. then the **second** 31. and the **third** took her, and likewise also the **seven** did not leave a child when they died. 32. Later the **wife** died also. 33. Therefore the **wife**, in the **resurrection**, whose **wife** does she become? For **seven** had her as **wife**." 34. Then **Y'shua** said to them, "The **children of this age** are marrying and being given in marriage, 35. and those of **that age**, and found worthy to reach the **resurrection of the dead**, neither **marry nor** are given in **marriage**: 36. for they are **not able to die again**, because they are like __angels__ and are **children of God**, being **children of the resurrection**. 37. But since the **dead are rising**, and **Moses revealed (this) at the bush**, as he said, 'Lord, the **God of Abraham** and (the) **God of Isaac** and (the) **God of Jacob**.' 38. Thus **He** is not (the) **God of (the) dead** but of (the) **living**, for **all** should be **living in Him**." (Exod. 3:6,15,16) 39. Then some of the scribes said, "Teacher, **You** said well." 40. For they were no longer daring to ask **Him** anything.*

In the Hereafter, all those who ENTER LIFE are like __Angels__ who are **not** physical beings. They appear to be humans, and are, but they do **Not** have physical parts! As verse thirty-eight says, they are **Living**. They are **Real**, but they are **Not** physical.

Rebellion

> Isaiah 14:12. *How you have **fallen from heaven**, O **shining son of the dawn**! How you, who did weaken the nations, are cut down to the ground! (Luke 10:18, Rev. 9:1; 12:9) 13. For you have said in your heart, **I shall ascend into heaven, I shall exalt my throne above the stars of God. I shall sit also upon the mountain of the con-***

gregation, in the recesses of the north. 14. I shall ascend above the heights of the clouds. I shall be like the Most High. 15. Yet you will be brought down to hell, to the lowest depth of the pit.

These verses tell of **Satan's** fall, kicked out of **Heaven** because of his **Rebellious attitude. Shining Son of the Dawn** is the **Hebrew** text, which was translated into **Latin** as **Lucifer**, meaning **Light Bringer**. The Hebrew word for **Nations** is **Goyim**, which also means **Heathens**, an apt name for the **followers of Satan. Heaven** has **no** place for them, so they will certainly **not** be **found** in **Heaven**.

No Rebellion will take place in Heaven, now or ever!

Jeremiah 6:16. *This is what the Lord says: Stand at the crossroads and look;* **ask for the ancient paths, ask where the good way is, and walk in it**, *and you will find rest for your souls. But you said, 'We will not walk in it.'* NIV

Jeremiah 6:16. *Thus says the LORD*, Stand in the roads! See!* **Ask for the old paths, Where is the good Way? Then walk there and you will find rest for your inner beings**. *But they said, We will not walk there.* ONMB

Sensing the full meaning of God's word requires help from the Holy Spirit. Only in the Spirit Realm will we have the full meaning of every passage.

PSALM 83

1. *A psalm of Asaf.*

2. **Do not cut Yourself off from me! Do not be silent! Do not be still, O God!**

3. *For, lo, Your enemies make a tumult, and those who hate You have lifted up their head.*

4. *They have taken deceitful counsel against Your people and consulted against Your protected ones.*

5. *They have said, Go! We will cut them off from being a nation, so the name of Israel may no longer be in remembrance.*

6. For they have consulted together with one consent. They are making a covenant against You, 7. the tents of Edom and the Ishmaelites, of Moab and the Hagrites, 8. Gebal and Ammon and Amalek, the Philistines with the inhabitants of Tyre, 9. and Ashur is joined with them: they have helped the children of Lot. Selah.

10. Do to them as to Midian; as to Sisera (Jdg. 4:21), as to Jabin (Jdg. 4:23,24) at the brook of Kishon, 11. who perished at Ein-Dor; they became dung for the earth.

12. Make their nobles like Oreb and like Zeeb (Jdg. 7:25), and all their princes like Zebah and Zalmuna (Jdg. 8:5-7) 13. who said, Let us take the pastures of God, land of Israel, in possession for ourselves.

*14. O my God, make them like a **whirl**, like the stubble before the **wind**.*

*15. As the fire burns **woods** and as the flame sets the **mountains** on fire; 16. so persecute them with Your tempest and terrify them with Your wind storm.*

This is a violent storm, destroying everything in its path - whether a wind storm, sandstorm, violent rain, blizzard, tornado, or hurricane; this could be translated as any of these. There will be **No** wind, **No** oxygen, **No** nitrogen, or **No** other gasses comparable to those making up the atmosphere on earth. **New Jerusalem** will not have any violence of any sort!

*Psalm 83:17. Fill their faces with **shame** so they will **seek Your name**, LORD*.*

*18. They will be confused and troubled forever, and they will be put to **shame** and **perish** 19. so they will know that You are the **Most High** over all the earth, Whose name alone is the **LORD***.*

Their **Shame** may well cause them to repent and seek the **LORD***. When the enemies are shamed, those Who do not seek the **LORD*** will Perish!

*Exodus 20:5. You will not bow yourself down to them, or serve them, for **I AM** the LORD* your God, a **jealous** God, visiting the iniquity of the fathers upon the children to the third and fourth generation of those who **hate Me**, 6. and showing **loving kindness** to thousands of those who love Me and keep My commandments.*

Jealousy is a trait reserved to be shown only to those who **Hate God**. These negative traits are listed here because they are not found in Heaven! The positive attributes are in the Chapter, The Wonderful Atmosphere in Heaven.

> Luke 9:46. *And a **thought came among them, whoever might be greatest of them**. 47. But since Y'shua saw the thought of their hearts, after He took hold of a child, He stood him beside Himself 48. and said to them, "Whoever would **take** this child in My name, **takes** Me: and whoever will **take** Me, is taking the **One Who sent Me**: for **the one who is least among you all, this one is great**."*

Every **Take** in Luke 9:47 means to **Take by the Hand**, meaning we are to really grab onto the things of God, being aggressive for Him. Matthew 11:12.

> *From the days of John the Immerser until now the **Kingdom of the Heavens** is taken by **violence**, and **shares in the Heavenly Kingdom** are sought for with the most ardent **Zeal** and the **most intense exertion** and **violent men** are **seizing it**, each one **claiming eagerly for himself**.*

Every believer is to have that kind of **zeal**, so **eager** to **seek God** and **please God**.

False Accusations

> Nehemiah 6.1. *Now it was, when Sanballat and Tobiah and Geshem the Arab and the rest of our enemies heard that I had built the wall, and that there was no breach left in it (though at that time I had not set up the doors in the gates) 2. that Sanballat and Geshem sent to me, saying, **Come, let us meet together in one of the villages in the plain of Ono**. But **they thought to destroy me**.*

Sanballat and Geshem planned to assassinate **Nehemiah**.

> Nehemiah 6:3. *And I sent messengers to them saying, "I am doing a great work, so that I cannot come down. Why should the work cease, while I leave it and come down to you?"*

Nehemiah 6:4. *Yet they sent to me **four times** after this sort and I answered them after the same manner. 5. Then Sanballat sent his servant to me in like manner the **fifth time with an open letter** in his hand 6. in which was written, It is reported among the nations and Gashmu (Geshem) says, **You and the Jews are thinking of rebellion**, for which cause you are building the wall, so you could be their **king**, according to these words. 7. And you have also appointed prophets to preach at Jerusalem saying, There is a king in Judah and now it will be reported to the king according to these words. Come now therefore and let us take counsel together.*

Blatant Lies will not exist in Heaven; There will be no deceit.

Nehemiah 6:8. *Then I sent to him saying, **There are no such things done such as you are saying, but you feign them out of your own heart.** 9. For they all put us in awe saying, Their hands will be weakened from the work, so it will not be done. Now therefore, strengthen my hands.*

Think about Eternal Life without any **negative emotions, no sadness, or grief**. There will be **no arguments or contention**! Those who want gun control should repent because there will be **no guns** in the Hereafter, **nor** any **anger** to cause the use of guns if any could be there.

The full list of physical things is so much longer that a complete list is too long to put here. This list will give you an idea:

All possessions, like cars, boats, bikes, furniture, houses, money, clothes, appliances, TVs, jewelry, lawns and gardens to tend, and whatever things to which you are attached.

Power to do Some Things Will Not be Used! With Satan Dead there will not be Evil things happening, so defensive powers will not be used.

The **Power** in the Spirit Realm is awesome, as we can see with the angels who brought Lot out of Sodom:

Genesis 19:11. *And they (the **angels**) **struck the men with blindness** that were at the door of the house, both small and great, so that*

57

*they wearied themselves to find the door. 12. And the men (**angels)** said to Lot, "Do you have here any besides yourself? Sons-in-law, your sons, your daughters, and whoever you have in the city; bring them out of this place, 13. for we will destroy this place, because their cry has become great before the face of the LORD*, and the LORD* has sent us to destroy it."*

This same **Spiritual Power** was later seen with **Elisha**:

*2 Kings 6:16. And he answered, **Do not be in awe!** For those who are with us are more than those with them. 17. And **Elisha** prayed and said, LORD*, now please, **open his eyes so he can see**. And the **LORD* opened the eyes of the young man**, and he **saw** and, there! The mountain was full of horses and chariots of fire all around **Elisha**. 18. And when they came down to him, **Elisha prayed to the LORD*** and said, **Strike this heathen people**, I pray you, with **blindness!** And **He** struck them with **blindness** according to the word of **Elisha**. 19. And **Elisha** said to them, This is **not** the **way**, neither is this the **city**. Follow me, and I shall bring you to the man whom you seek. And he led them to **Samaria**.*

*20. And it was, when they had come into **Samaria** that **Elisha** said, **LORD*, open the eyes** of these men so they can see. And the **LORD* opened their eyes** and they **saw** and, behold, they were in the midst of **Samaria**. 21. And the king of Israel said to **Elisha** when he saw them, My father, will I strike them? Will I strike them, my father?*

Elisha then says to set 'Bread and Water before them, which means to give them a Meal, more than just Bread and Water.

*2 Kings 6:22. And he answered, You will **not strike them**. Would you strike those whom you have taken captive with your sword and with your bow? Set bread and water before them, so they can eat and drink and go to their master. 23. And he prepared **great provision** for them, and when they had eaten and had drunk he sent them away and they went to their master. So the bands of Syria no longer came into the land of Israel.*

Elijah had earlier shown **Spiritual Power** to call down **Fire from Heaven:**

1 Kings 18:30. *And **Elijah** said to all the people, Come near to me. And all the people came near to him. And he repaired the altar of the LORD* that was broken down. 31. And Elijah took twelve stones, according to the number of the tribes of the sons of Jacob, to whom the word of the LORD* came saying, Israel will be your name. 32. And he built an altar with the stones in the name of the LORD*, and he made a trench around the altar, as great as would hold two measures of seed. 33. And he put the wood in order and cut the bull in pieces and laid it on the wood 34. and he said, **Fill four jars with water and let them pour it on the burnt offering and on the wood**. And he said, Do it the second time. And they did it the **second time**. And he said, Do it the **third time**. And they did it the **third time**. 35. And the water ran over the altar, and he also filled the trench with water.*

The Fire of the LORD* Confirms Elijah

1 Kings 18:36. *And it was at the time of the afternoon burnt offering that **Elijah** the prophet came near and said, LORD* God of Abraham, Isaac, and of Israel, let it be known this day that You are God in Israel, and that I am Your servant and I have done all these things at Your word. 37. Answer me, LORD*. Answer me, so this people can know that You are the LORD* God, and You have turned their heart back again. 38. Then **the fire of the LORD* fell and consumed the burnt sacrifice, the wood, the stones, the dust, and licked up the water that was in the trench**.*

Elijah Does it Again:

2 Kings 1:9. *Then the king sent to him a captain of fifty with his fifty. And he went up to him and, behold, he was sitting on the top of a hill. And he spoke to him, You! Man of God, the king has said, Come down! 10. And **Elijah** answered and said to the captain of fifty, If I am a man of God, then **let fire come down from heaven and consume you and your fifty**. And fire from heaven came down and consumed him and his fifty. 11. And again he sent **another captain of fifty with his fifty to him**. And he answered and said to him, O man of*

*God, thus has the king said, Come down quickly! And Elijah answered and said to them, **If I am a man of God, let fire come down from heaven and consume you and your fifty**. And the **fire of God came down from heaven and consumed him and his fifty**.*

The **Awesome Power** to call down Fire from Heaven will **Never** be used in the Hereafter because there will be no demonic forces to fight! Elijah and Elisha showed us the **Power** that we have in the **Spirit** while we are on earth, but that **Power** will never be needed in Heaven. The Church could and should use the **Power** that has been made available to us, but most of the Church is asleep at the switch, not even aware that the **Power** is available.

Y'shua showed even more examples of **Power**, but those too will never be needed or used in Heaven!

Power to Raise the Dead:

John 11:38. ***Y'shua*** *then again, being deeply moved within Himself, came to the tomb: and it was a cave and a stone was lying upon it. 39. **Y'shua** said, "You must remove the stone." Martha, the sister of the one who had died, said to Him, "Lord, he already has an odor, for it has been four days." 40. **Y'shua** said to her, "Did I not say that if you would believe you would see the glory of God?" 41. Then they removed the stone. And **Y'shua** looked up and said, "Father, I give You thanks because You heard Me. 42. And I have known that You always hear Me, but I spoke because of the crowd that was standing around, so that they would believe that You sent Me." 43. And after He said these things He cried out in a loud voice, **"Lazarus, come outside."** 44. The one who died came out, although his feet and hands had been bound with strips of cloth and his face was bound with a face cloth. Y'shua said to them, "You must **loose** him at once and you must **allow him to go**."*

This is a Hebrew poetic parallelism for emphasis, with **loose** an idiom meaning to permit, **allow**.

The Healing of a Mute Person

> Matthew 9:32. *And while they were coming out behold they brought to **Him** a man who had a deaf and mute demon. 33. Then after **He cast out the demon the mute man spoke.** And the crowds were amazed saying, **"Never has this been known in Israel."***

Deliverance and **Healing** will be **unknown in Heaven** because **they** are the weapons against **Evil Forces**, forces that do not exist in Heaven.

> Matthew 10.1. *Then after He summoned His twelve disciples **He gave them authority over unclean spirits, so that they could cast them out and heal every disease and every sickness.** 2. And the names of the twelve apostles were these, first Simon, the one called Peter, and Andrew his brother, and **Jacob** the son of Zebedee, and John his brother, 3. Philip and Bartholomew, Thomas and Matthew the tax collector, **Jacob** the son of Alpheus, and Thaddaeus, 4. Simon the Zealot, and Judas from Iscariot, the one who gave Him over.*

The name in the Greek text is Iakob, Jacob in English.

No Kingdom Preaching in Heaven!

> Matthew 10:5. ***Y'shua** sent these twelve, after He commanded them, saying, "On the way **do not go to the heathens and do not enter a Samaritan city: 6. but you must rather go regularly to the <u>lost sheep</u> of the House of Israel.** 7. And while you are going you must preach, saying that **'The Kingdom of the <u>Heavens</u> has come near.'** 8. You must continually **heal sicknesses, raise (the) dead, cleanse lepers, cast out demons**: you took freely, you must now give freely.*

There will be **No lost sheep** in Heaven! Heavens is always plural in Hebrew. See **Heavens** in Glossary. This is **not** the disease known as **leprosy** today. See **Leprosy** in Glossary.

> Matthew 10:9. *You can acquire neither **gold** nor **silver** nor **copper** in your belts, 10. nor a knapsack for (the) way nor two tunics nor sandals nor a staff: for the worker is worthy of his food. 11. In whatever city or town you would enter you must at once examine (to determine)*

who in it is worthy: remain there in (that house) until whenever you would leave. 12. And when you enter a house you must immediately greet it: 13. then if the house would be worthy, your peace must come upon it: but if it would not be worthy, your peace must return to you. 14. And whoever would not take you in and would not listen to your message, when you come outside the house or that city you must right away shake off the dust from your feet. 15. Truly I say to you, it will be more bearable in the region of Sodom and Gomorra on Judgment Day than in that city."

In Heaven, there will be **no Gold, Silver, or Copper; nor** will there be evangelizing, since all the sinners will be in the Second Death; there is **no** Money, **no** Silver, **no** Copper, **no** Gold. Everything in Heaven is **Spiritual, Not** Physical! There is **no** Evil to be overcome; there is **nothing Evil** in Heaven! The verb **Take** means to **Take by the hand**, meaning to give them a **warm welcome**.

No Persecution iin Heaven!

Matthew 10:16. *"Behold I am sending you as **sheep** in the midst of **wolves**: therefore you must become as **prudent** as **serpents** and as **innocent** as **doves**. 17. And you must be on guard from men: for they will give you over to Sanhedrins (**courts**) and they will scourge you in their public gatherings: 18. and you will be led before rulers and even kings because of Me, in witness to them and to the heathens. 19. And when they would arrest you, **do not be anxious how or what you would say**: for what you should say **will be given to you at that moment**: 20. for you will not be those speaking but (it will be) the **Spirit** of your **Father**, the **One Who speaks through you**. 21. And a brother will betray a brother into death and a father a child, and children will rise up in rebellion against parents and **they will put them to death**. (Mic. 7:6) 22. And you will be hated by all because of **My name**: but the one who has persevered to (the) end will be saved. 23. And when they would pursue you in this city, you must flee to another: for truly I say to you, you would not finish the cities of Israel until the Son of Man would come.*

There is persecution of Christians and Jews throughout the world today.

HEAVEN'S WONDERFUL ATMOSPHERE 4

The wonderful attributes of the LORD*, saying that we who are made in His Image will make Heaven, well, Heaven!

> Genesis 1:26. *Then God said,* **"We will make mankind in our image, after our likeness and have dominion over the fish of the sea, over the fowl of the air, over the cattle, over all the earth, and over every creeping thing that creeps upon the earth."** 27. *So God created mankind in His own image; He created him in the image of God. He created them male and female.*

Mankind has been made in the physical image of God, as is seen whenever God has appeared on Earth – like He did to Abraham:

> Luke 24:36. *And while they were saying these things He stood in the midst of them and said to them, "Shalom Aleichem,"*

Y'shua promised that no good thing would be withheld.

The Seventh Seal Brings Temporary Silence:

> Revelation 8.1. *And when He opened the* **seventh seal,** *there was* **silence in heaven for about half an hour.** 2. *And I saw the seven angels who stood before God, and seven trumpets were given to them.*

There will be **Music and Singing constantly** in Heaven, except only for this one time that Scripture mentions **Silence** in Heaven.

Psalm 57:6. ***Be exalted, O God, above the heavens! Your glory is over all the earth!***

This Psalm will continually ring out clearly!

Isaiah 61.1. *The **Spirit of Adonai, the LORD*, is upon me**, because the **LORD* has anointed me to preach Good News to the humble**. (Matt. 5:3) He has sent me **to bind up the broken-hearted, to proclaim liberty to the captives, and opening of eyes (Isa. 42:7) for those who are bound**, 2. **to proclaim the acceptable year of the LORD***, (Luke 4:18-20) and the day of vengeance of our God; to comfort all who mourn, (Matt. 5:4) 3. **to appoint to those who mourn in Zion, to give to them beauty instead of ashes, the oil of joy instead of mourning, the garment of praise (prayer shawl) instead of the spirit of infirmity**, so they could be **called oaks of righteousness**, the planting of the LORD*, so He would be glorified.*

Opening of eyes, the Hebrew word **Hippatach**, means the **opening of eyes and ears** both **literally and Spiritually**. Spirit of Infirmity, the Hebrew word Kehah, literally means to be pale or dim, and it is used as an expression for feeling weak or sickly. The people addressed by Isaiah are called **oaks** as the **opposite of weak, sickly**.

Isaiah 60.1. ***Arise, and give Light!*** *For your **Light has come**, and the **Glory of the LORD* has shone (like the sun) upon you**. 2. For, behold, the darkness will cover the earth and gross darkness the people, but the LORD* will **rise** (like the sun) upon you, and His glory will be seen upon you. (Rev. 21:11) 3. And nations will come to your **Light**, and kings to the brightness of your **rising** (like the sun). (Rev. 21:24)*

The Hebrew verb **Zarah**, translated Shine, refers to the Sun because Zarah is used only for the **rising** of the **sun;** Zarah is also used in Isaiah 60:2-3.

Luke 2:8. *And **shepherds** were in this field, living out of doors and keeping watch by night over their flock. 9. And an **angel** of the Lord appeared to them and the glory of the Lord **shone** around them, and they feared a great fear. 10. Then the **angel** said to them, "You must not be afraid, for behold **I have good news for you**, great **joy** which* *will be for all the people, 11. because this day in the city of David a* **Savior was born** *for you, Who is* **Messiah, Lord***. 12. And this will be a sign to you, you will find an infant wrapped and lying in a stall." 13. Then suddenly there were with the* **angel** *a great number of the* **heavenly hosts praising God** *and saying,*

14. **"Glory to God in the highest**

and on Earth peace and good will among men."

The Heavenly Hosts are literally "the soldiers of Heaven." The **Savior**, the **Messiah**, was born in a cave near the **Tower of the Flock. Tower of the Flock, Migdal Eder** in Hebrew, refers to the **Tower** in fields near Bethlehem which sheltered the **Shepherds** and from which they watched over the **Lambs**. There the **Lambs** were cared for that were to become the **Lambs** offered in the Temple, kept by Levitical Priests. The Aaronite priests offered two **Lambs** every day, one in the morning and one in the evening. Each **Lamb** had to be **unblemished, perfect**. Each **Lamb** was offered to **take away the sins of the people,** so it is no wonder that this is the place the **LORD*** chose for the birth of His **Incarnate Body**.

Psalm 65:5. *Blessed is the man whom You choose, and cause to approach You, so he can dwell in Your courts. We will be* **satisfied** *with the goodness of* **Your House,** *of* **Your holy Temple.**

Yes, LORD*, we will be **satisfied** forever!

Luke 8:2. *And He said to them,* **"My mother and My brothers are these who hear and do the Word of God."**

The only **Word of God** when **Y'shua** said this was the **Hebrew Scriptures.** Those who **hear** and **do** the **Word of God** will be the occupants of **Heaven,** and they will all have the **Fruit of the Spirit!**

Galatians 5:22. *But the* **fruit of the Spirit** *is* **love joy peace, patience kindness goodness, faithfulness** *23.* **gentleness self-control***: there is nothing (in) Torah (Teaching) against such as these. 24. But those who belong to* **Messiah Y'shua** *did crucify their flesh with (its) passions and desires. 25. If we live by (the) Spirit, then we walk, directing our lives by (the) Spirit. 26. We should not become boastful, (neither) provoking one another, (nor) envying one another.*

All those in Heaven will continuously demonstrate the **Fruit of the Spirit**, always having crucified their flesh, not bringing any of our earthly life's passions with its lusts and desires.

> Nehemiah 8:10. *Then he said to them, Go your way, eat **delicacies** and drink the sweet and send portions to those for whom nothing is prepared, for this day is holy unto our Lord!* ***Do not be grieved, for the joy of the LORD* is your strength!***

Delicacies are rich, fatty, sweet foods. Some translations say "eat the fat.." but that is misleading since the fat in these foods is olive oil, not animal fat. This is the **Feast of Sukkot**, a day for **feasting**, not fasting. **Messiah Y'shua** and **the LORD*** are **One**, so all who are faithful to the **LORD*** have the above attributes, making Heaven, **Heaven!**

> Matthew 18:4. *Therefore whoever will **humble himself** like this **child**, this one is the **greatest** in the Kingdom of the **Heavens**. 5. And whoever would take one such child in My name, **takes Me**."*

Not one in Heaven will want to take the limelight, with everyone there being **Humble!**

> Genesis 18:1. ***And the LORD* appeared*** *to him in the plains of Mamre and he was sitting in the tent door in the heat of the day. 2. And he lifted up his eyes and looked, and **there were three men standing by him**. And when he saw them, he ran from the tent door to meet them and he bowed toward the ground 3. and said, "My Lord, if now I have found favor in Your sight, do not pass by, I pray **You**, from **Your** servant: 4. let a little water, I pray you, be brought and wash your feet and rest yourselves under the tree. 5. And I shall get a morsel of bread and comfort your hearts for you. After that you will pass on, for that is why you have come to your servant." And they said, "So do as you have said." 6. And Abraham hastened into the tent to Sarah and said, "Make ready quickly three measures of fine meal, knead it and make cakes." 7. And Abraham ran to the herd and fetched a good, tender calf and gave it to a young man and he hastened to dress it. 8. And he took butter, milk, and the calf which he had dressed and set it before them, and he stood by them under the tree and they ate.*

We also are made in **His emotional image**, having the same emotions that God has! The negative emotions are named in the Introduction, but those will not be carried over into the Hereafter. Heaven will not have any Evil influence; there will be **no** worship of Strange gods, **no** cursing, **no** jealousy, **no** grief, and **no** other **bad thing** in **Heaven**. **Love** will flow from **everyone in Heaven**.

> Numbers 23:6. *Nevertheless the **LORD*** your **God** would **not** listen to **Balaam**, but the **LORD*** your **God** turned the curse into a blessing for you, because the **LORD*** your **God loved you**.*

Balaam was offered Riches by Balak to curse Israel, but the **LORD*** continually **Blessed Israel. His attributes** will be **ever-present**.

> Exodus 34:5. *And the LORD* descended in the cloud and stood with him there and proclaimed the name of the LORD*. 6. And the LORD* passed by before him and proclaimed, "The LORD*, the LORD* God,* **compassionate** *and* **gracious, patient,** *and* **abundant in loving kindness and truth,** *7. keeping* **loving kindness** *for thousands,* **forgiving iniquity, transgression, and sin,***

In verse three, **You** and **Your** are capitalized because they are singular, referring specifically to God, showing that Abraham knew he was being visited by God. The other two visitors were angels, who also looked like men; we are made in His image!

All believers are to lead in showing **Love, Compassion, Graciousness, Patience, Loving Kindness,** and **Forgiveness** to **everyone** to bring more people into the Kingdom. Our behavior is to attract others so they will become believers in the **Holy God**!

> Leviticus 19:18. *You will not avenge or bear any grudge against the children of your people, but you will **love** your neighbor as yourself. I AM the **LORD*!***

Love is the dominant emotion in Heaven, with no one following false gods!

> Exodus 20:5. *You will not bow yourself down to them, or serve them, for **I AM** the LORD* your God, a jealous God, visiting the iniquity of*

*the fathers upon the children to the third and fourth generation of those who hate Me, 6. and showing **loving kindness** to thousands of those who love Me and keep My commandments.*

Everything we do will be done in **Love.**

Zephaniah 3:16. *In that Day it will be said to Jerusalem, **Do not be in awe!** To Zion, **Do not let your hands be slack!** 17. The LORD* your God is mighty in your midst! He will deliver! He will **rejoice enthusiastically** over you with **joy!** He will rest in His **love**, He will **rejoice** over you with **singing**.*

Our **Rejoicing** and our **Worship** will be enthusiastic. We will **Laugh** with expressive **Joy**!

Isaiah 25:9. *And it will be said in that **day**, Lo, this is our God. We have waited for Him and He will save us. This is the **LORD***! We have waited for **Him**. We will **rejoice exuberantly** and be **glad** in His deliverance/salvation.*

Isaiah 29:19. *The **Humble (Repentant)** also will increase (their) **joy** in the **LORD***, and the **Humble (Repentant)** among men will **rejoice enthusiastically** in the Holy One of Israel.*

Heaven will be filled with People Rejoicing Enthusiastically! All the Saints will be like Jeremiah when we take nourishment from the Word of God.

Jeremiah 15:16. ***Your Words** were found and **I ate them**, and **Your Word** was to me the **Joy** and **Rejoicing** of my heart, for I am called by Your name, **LORD***, **God of Hosts**.*

Psalm 1:1. *Blessed is the man who does not walk in the counsel of the ungodly, or stand in the way of sinners, or sit in the seat of the scornful. 2. But his **Delight** is in the **Torah (Teaching)** of the **LORD*** and he meditates on His Torah (Teaching) both day and night.*

Everyone in Heaven will **Delight** in the food! There will be **NO** indigestion, **NO** turning up noses at the **Delightful** meals we will have as we devour the **Word of God**.

Psalm 37:13. *The Lord will* **laugh** *at him for He sees that his day is coming.*

Psalm 144:15. **Happy** *is that people that is in such a state: yea,* **Happy** *is that people, whose God is the* **LORD***.*

In that delightful atmosphere, we will even recline!

Psalm 125:2. 2. *As the mountains are round about Jerusalem, so the* **LORD*** *is round about His people, from now and forevermore*.

Now in the physical realm, the LORD* is like the mountains, round about Jerusalem, but in the Hereafter, with no physical mountains, He will continue to be round about us. **New Jerusalem** will be so large, especially with its height being 1,500 miles, that there will be mountain chains, with snow-capped peaks always in sight. The **Spiritual nature** will always be comfortable because the snow itself is spiritual; Everything will be **Spiritual**, the mountains, lakes, the forests, the roads, and any animals found there.

Matthew 8:11. *I say to you that many will come from east and west and* **will recline** *with Abraham, Isaac, and Jacob in the* **Kingdom of the Heavens**,

All those in Heaven will recline to eat the Word of God!

Luke 24:13. *Then behold this day* **two of them were going to a distant village**; *it was named* **Emmaus**, *sixty stadia (about seven miles) from Jerusalem. 14. And they were speaking with one another about all these happenings. 15. And it was, while they were speaking and discussing (these things) that Y'shua Himself, having approached, was going with them 16. but* **their eyes were being hindered** *(so) they did* **not recognize Him**. *17. And* **He** *said to them, "What are these accounts which you are exchanging with one another while you are walking?" And they stood still, (being) sad and gloomy. 18. And one named* **Cleopas** *said to* **Him**, *"Are You the only one living in Jerusalem and not knowing what happened in her during these days?" 19. And* **He** *said to them, "Of what sort?" And they said to* **Him**, *"The things about*

*Y'shua of Nazareth, **Who** was a man, a prophet powerful in work and in word, in the presence of God and of all the people, 20. how our high priests and our leaders gave **Him** over in judgment of death and **they crucified Him**. 21. But **we were hoping that He was the One Who was going to redeem Israel**: but even with all these things, this third day has passed since these things happened. 22. And even some of our women amazed us, since they came to the tomb early in the morning, 23. and when they did not find **His** body, they came saying then that in a vision they saw angels, who were saying 'He is alive.' 24. Then some of those with us left for the tomb and also found thus just as the women said, but they did not see **Him**." 25. But **He** said to them, "O **foolish and slow in heart to believe all that the prophets were saying**: 26. for was it not **necessary** for the **Messiah to suffer these things**, then to enter **His glory**?" 27. And beginning with Moses and with all the Prophets He explained to them with all the **writings concerning Himself**.*

Everyone in Heaven will rejoice as they consume the Word of God!

The names of Cleopas and Clopas are very clear when we examine the Greek names: The Greek spelling of **Cleopas** is **Kleopas**, while the spelling of **Clopas**, John 19:25, is **Klopa**. The "K" letters were changed to "C"s by the Latin language, from which the first English Bibles were translated. In Greek, the "**O**" in **Klopa** is an **Omega**, while the "**O**" in **Kleopas** is an **Omicron**. Both words are in the **genitive case**, with **Klopa** masculine and **Kleopas** feminine. His disciples were expecting the **reigning Messiah immediately**. Numerous Scholars think **Kleopas** was **Peter's wife.**

Y'shua says the blessing over the meal; then, their eyes are opened.

Luke 24:28. *Then they approached the village to which they were going, and **He** pretended to go farther on. 29. But they urged **Him** saying, "You must now stay with us because it is toward evening and the day is already over." And **He** came in to stay with them. 30. And it happened while **He** reclined with them, when **He** took the bread **He** **praised God** and after **He** broke (it) **He** gave (it) to them, 31. and **their eyes were opened** and **they recognized Him**: then **He became invisible** for them. 32. And they said to one another, "Was not* *our heart burning in us as **He** was speaking to us on the way, as **He** was explaining the Scriptures to us?" 33. Then after they got up they returned to **Jerusalem** the same hour and found the eleven and those gathered with them, 34. saying that truly the Lord had risen and was seen by **Simon**. 35. And they were recounting the things discussed (by **Y'shua**) on the way and as **He** was recognized by them while **He** was breaking the bread.*

They returned from **Emmaus**, so the round trip was about fourteen miles in the afternoon and evening, showing their being in good shape from all the walking they had been doing. In **His spirit body, with no flesh, He could be invisible.** There is **no flesh** in the **Spirit Realm.** So, at this meeting, **Y'shua** was in both the **real World** and the **Spirit Realm.** When **He** was in the **natural World, He** controlled whether **He** was in the **Natural** or in the **Spirit.** In verse thirty-four, **Simon** is clarified by **Paul** in **1 Corinthians 15:5** as **Peter, not Simon the Zealot**, as one of the disciples walking with **Him** to **Emmaus.** Verse eighteen names **Cleopas** as the other disciple. While most people assume **Cleopas** is a man, the Greek spelling has a **feminine genitive** (possessive) ending, so numerous scholars speculate that this could have been **Peter's wife** on the road to **Emmaus** with him.

His Appearance to the Disciples

Luke 24:36. *And while they were saying these things **He** stood in the midst of them and said to them, "**Shalom Aleichem,**" ("Peace (be) with you.") 37. But becoming terrified and afraid they were thinking that they saw a spirit. 38. Then **He** said to them, "Why are you disturbed and why are the doubts going up in your heart? 39. You must now look at **My** hands and **My** feet because I AM **He**: you must now touch **Me** and see, because **a spirit does not have flesh and bone just as you see Me having.**" 40. Then having said this **He** showed them **His** hands and feet. 41. But they still did not believe from the joy, and marveling **He** said to them, "Do you have something here to eat?" 42. And they gave **Him** a portion of **broiled fish**: 43. then after **He** took (it) **He** ate in front of them.*

In the natural world, **Y'shua** had both a Physical and a Spirit Body, but in the **Spirit Realm, He** only has a **Spirit Body**, just as we will have only **Spirit**

Bodies in **Heaven**. Everything in **Heaven** is **Spirit**! Although everything is **Spirit**, everything is also **Real, just not Physical**!

> Luke 24:44. *And **He** said to them, "These (are) the messages I told you while I was still with you, that it is necessary for everything to be fulfilled that has been written about **Me** in the Torah (Teaching) of Moses and in the Prophets and the Psalms." 45. Then **He opened their __minds__** and they **understood the Scriptures**: 46. and **He** said to them that "Thus it has been written that the **Messiah** would **suffer** (Isaiah 53:5) and be raised from the dead on the **third day**, 47. and **repentance** would be preached in **His name** for **forgiveness of sins** for all the **heathens**. Beginning from Jerusalem 48. you (are) witnesses of these things. 49. Then behold, **I, Myself**, am sending My Father's **promise** upon you: but you must now stay in the city until you would be clothed in power from on high."*

Y'shua then explains His appearance.

The **promise** is the **Immersion** (Baptism) of the **Holy Spirit**, given for the first time in Acts 2:1-12, from Joel 3:1-3.

The Coming of the Holy Spirit

> Acts 2.1. *And when the day of **Shavuot** had come they were all in one place together. 2. And a sound came suddenly out of heaven as bringing a violent wind and it filled the whole **House** where they were sitting 3. and dividing tongues like fire were seen by them and the flames sat upon each one of them, 4. and **all** were **filled by the Holy Spirit** and began to **speak in other languages** just as the **Spirit** was giving them to speak out boldly.*

Shavuot is the Feast of **Weeks**, seven **Weeks** after **First Fruits** in the Feast of Passover. **House** often refers to the **Temple**. "The House" is frequently used in Hebrew when speaking of the **Temple,** and here the South steps of the **Temple** were one of the few places in Jerusalem where thousands could gather, sitting on the steps of Solomon's Porch. The streets were too narrow and the houses too small for such a large crowd. Few houses would have had a room that could hold over one hundred people. Luke also refers to the **Sanctuary** as "**the House**" in Luke 11:51.

*Acts 2:5. And there were Jewish people staying in Jerusalem, devout people from all the nations under heaven. 6. And when this **sound** was made a multitude gathered and was amazed, because while they were speaking, **they all were hearing in their own languages.** 7. And they were astounded and amazed saying, "Look, are not all those who are speaking from Galilee? 8. Then how do we each hear in our own language with which we were born? 9. **Parthians** and **Medes** and **Elamites** and those who dwell in **Mesopotamia**, **Judea**, and even **Cappadocia**, **Pontus**, and **Asia**, 10. **Phrygia**, and also **Pamphylia**, **Egypt** and the parts of **Libya** around **Cyrene**, and the visiting **Romans**, 11. **Cretes** and **Arabs**, both **Jewish** people and **proselytes.** We hear them speaking the **greatness of God in our languages.**" 12. And all were amazed and perplexed, saying to one another, "What does this mean?" 13. But others, mocking, were saying, "They are drunk because they have been filled with sweet new wine."*

In verse nine, **Cappadocia** is an inland region of Asia Minor, referred to as **Gamadim** in Ezekiel 27:11.

Peter's Speech at Shavuot

*Acts 2:14. But **Peter**, as he stood up with the eleven, raised his voice and spoke out to them, "**Men, Jewish people**, and **all those who are visiting Jerusalem**, let this be known to you and pay attention to my words. 15. For these are not drunk as you assume, for it is (the) **third hour of the day**,*

The **third hour of the Day** was **9:00 AM**, the time of **Morning Prayer**.

*Acts 2:16. but **this is that which was spoken through the prophet Joel**,*

Joel 3:1. *And it will be afterward that **I shall pour out My Spirit** upon all flesh and your **sons and your daughters will prophesy**, your **old men will dream dreams**, your **young men will see visions**, 2. and **I shall pour out My Spirit** also upon the **servants** and upon the **hand maidens** in those days, 3. and I shall show **wonders** in the **heavens** and in the **earth**, **blood** and **fire** and **pillars of smoke**.*

73

The **Pouring out of His Spirit** has brought speaking in **tongues**, **miracles**, **healings**, **prophesying**, **visions**, and **dreams**, often unexpected by those who are given the gifts. **Shavuot**, meaning **Weeks**, is often called by its Greek name, Pentecost. In Acts 2:15, the third hour of the day is 9:00 AM, the time of morning prayer and the morning sacrifice.

The Spirit Enters Ezekiel

Ezekiel 2.1. *And He said to me, Son of man, stand upon your feet and I shall speak to you. 2. And the* **Spirit entered me** *when* **He** *spoke to me and set me upon my feet, so I heard* **Him Who** *spoke to me. 3. And* **He** *said to me, Son of man,* **I AM sending you** *to the* **children of Israel**, *to a rebellious nation that has rebelled against* **Me**. *They and their fathers have transgressed against* **Me**, *to this very day. 4. For they are impudent children and stiff hearted. I AM sending you to them and you will say to them, The word of* **Adonai**, *the* **LORD***. *5. And they, whether they will hear, or whether they will hold back, (for they are a* **rebellious house**) *will yet know that there has been a prophet among them.*

Ezekiel told to ignore the Rebellious advisors:

Ezekiel 2:6. *And you, son of man,* **Do not be in awe of them! Do not be in awe of their words!** *You are among briers and thorns and you live among scorpions.* **Do not be in awe of their words! Do not be dismayed at their looks!** *They are a rebellious house. 7. And you will speak My words to them, whether they will hear or whether they will cease, for they are most rebellious.*
8. But you, son of man, Listen! Obey what I AM says to you! **Do not be rebellious like that rebellious house!** *Open your mouth and eat what I AM is giving you. (Rev. 10:9)*
9. And when I looked, behold, a hand was sent to me and, lo, a scroll of a book was there. (Rev. 10:9) 10. And He spread it before me and it was written on both sides and lamentations and mourning and woe were written there. (Rev. 5:1)

Ezekiel told to Eat the Scroll

3:4. And He said to me, Son of man, **go to the House of Israel to speak to them with My words**. *5. For you are not sent to a people of* *an obscure speech and of a hard language, but to the* **House of Israel***, 6. not to many peoples of an obscure speech and of a hard language, whose words you cannot understand. Surely, had I sent you to them, they would have listened to you. 7. But the* **House of Israel will not listen to you***, for* **they will not listen to Me***, for the* **whole House of Israel is impudent and hard hearted***. 8. Behold, I have made your face strong against their faces and your forehead strong against their foreheads. 9. I have made your forehead like an adamant harder than flint.* **Do not be in awe of them** *or* **be dismayed at their looks***, for they are a* **rebellious house***.*

10. Moreover He said to me, Son of man, **take in your heart all My words** *that I shall speak to you and hear with your ears. 11. Then go! Come to those of the* **captivity***, to the* **children of your people***! Speak to them and tell them, whether they will listen or whether they will not listen, Thus says* **Adonai***, the* **LORD****.*

Like Ezekiel, we are to eat the **Word of God,** which will feed us in **Eternal Life.** Remember you are what you eat, including what you watch on TV, what you read, what you talk about, what you listen to, and what you think about! Your food in Heaven will only be the **Word of God!**

Know that what Ezekiel writes in **chapter Nine** is real, and it is spiritual, not physical! Your behavior determines whether you have the mark of the Saints.

Ezekiel 9.1. *Then He cried in my ears with a loud voice saying, Cause those who have charge over the city to draw near, even every man with his destroying weapon in his hand. 2. And, behold, six men came from the road of the higher gate, which lies toward the north and* **each man a slaughter weapon in his hand***, and* **one man among them was clothed with linen, with a writer's inkhorn by his side***. And they went in and stood beside the bronze altar. 3. And the* **glory of the God of Israel** *went up from the cherub, upon which it was, to the threshold of the House. And He called to the man* **clothed in linen***, who had the* **writer's inkhorn** *by his side.*

Mark the Saint

Ezekiel 9:4. *And the LORD* said to him, Go through the midst of the city, through the midst of Jerusalem, and <u>**set a mark**</u> upon the **foreheads** of the people who **sigh and who cry over all the abominations that are done in its midst**.* (Rev. 7:3; 9:4; 14:1; 22:4) 5. *And to the others He said in my hearing,*

Strike the Sinner

Go after him through the city, and <u>strike</u>! **Do not let your eye spare! Do not have pity!** *6. You (pl) will slay completely old and young, virgins, little children, and women!* **Do not come near anyone upon whom is the mark!**

Do not spare and Do not have pity! These are two very strong commands, not permitting any emotional reaction to soften the punishment. All who do not have Mark on the forehead will be struck and killed by the six executioners.

Begin at My Sanctuary

<u>*Begin at My Sanctuary*</u>*. Then they began with the* **elders** *who were in front of the House. 7. And He said to them, Defile the House and fill the courts!* **Begin at My Sanctuary** *with the* **slain.** *Go forth! And they went forth and slew in the city. 8. And it was, while they were slaying them, and I was left, that I fell upon my face and cried and said, Ah* **Adonai, LORD***! *Will You destroy all the residue of Israel in Your pouring out of Your fury upon Jerusalem?*

9. Then He said to me, The **iniquity of the House of Israel and Judah** *is exceeding great and the land is full of blood and the city full of perversity for they say, The* **LORD*** *has forsaken the earth and the* **LORD*** *does not see. 10. And as for* **Me also, My eye will not spare, neither will I have pity**, *but I will pay back their way upon their head. 11. And see, the man clothed in linen, who had the ink well by his side reported the matter saying,* **I have done** *as* **You** *have commanded me.*

The above report by Ezekiel is what will happen as **Judgment Day** unfolds, the mark on the forehead being **Spiritual**!

> Ezekiel 37.1. *The hand of the **LORD*** *was upon me and carried me out in the **Spirit** of the **LORD*** *and set me down in the midst of the valley which was full of **bones**, 2. and caused me to pass by them all around and, behold, there were very many in the open valley and, lo, they were very dry. 3. And **He** said to me, Son of man, can these **bones** live?*

Ezekiel was in the **Spirit**, so this is in the **Hereafter,** where there will **NOT** be any **Bones**. The **Hereafter** will be **Spiritual**! There will **NOT** be **any Bones, any Flesh, any Air, any Water, any Trees, any Animals**, although all those will exist in the **Spirit,** and they will be **REAL**; they will not be **Physical**.

> Ezekiel 37:4. *Again **He** said to me, Prophesy over, (in the direction of these bones) and say to **them**, (the **people**), O you **dry bones**, Listen! **Obey the word of the LORD***! 5. *Thus says **Adonai**, the **LORD*** *to-ward these **bones**, Behold, I AM will cause **breath to enter you and you will live**, (Rev. 11:11) 6. and I shall lay sinews upon you and will bring up flesh upon you and cover you with skin and put a **Spirit** in you, and you **will live**, and you **will know that I AM the LORD***.

The pronoun '**them**' in verse four does not refer to **bones** but to the **people** who formerly used the bones. **Bones**, 'atsam'ot' in Hebrew is a **feminine** noun, while the **pronoun** 'alaihem' is **masculine**. **All** the **pronouns** in verses 5, 6, 8, through 14, every "**you**" is **masculine plural**. That means this passage is **allegorical**, **not literal**.

> Ezekiel 37:7. *So I prophesied as I was commanded and as I prophesied, there was a noise and behold a shaking and the **bones** came together, **bone** to its **bone**. 8. And when I looked, lo, the sinews and the flesh came upon them, (the people), and the skin covered them above, but there was **no breath** in them. 9. Then He said to me, Prophesy to the wind, prophesy, son of man, and say to the wind, Thus says **Adonai**, the **LORD***, Come from the four winds, O breath, and **breathe** upon these slain, so they can **live**.* (Rev. 7:1)

77

This all happened in the **Spirit!** There will be no **physical bodies** in **Heaven!** In the 1980s, Evangelist Jesse Duplantis spoke about his visit to **Heaven.** When he **walked** on **flowers,** the **flowers,** which were **Spirit,** came through his **feet;** he did **not trample** the **flowers** because his **spirit body** had **no flesh, no bones, no weight. Neither** will our **Spirit bodies** have any **Bones or Weight** when we get to **Heaven.** The **flowers** were **not** affected by his **weightless Spirit body.**

He also **saw God** as a huge glow of **His Glory!** That matches what the Israelites saw in Exodus 24.

> Exodus 24:9. *Then Moses and Aaron, Nadab and Abihu, and seventy of the elders of Israel went up. 10. And **they saw the God of Israel and there was under His feet as it were a paved work of brilliant sapphire** (Ezek. 1:26, Rev. 4:2) and as it were the **body of heaven in its clearness.** 11. And He did not lay His hand upon the **nobles of the children of Israel: they also** <u>saw God</u>, then they ate and drank.*

All the **Elders** of the Children of Israel **saw God** without being destroyed. What they saw, **His feet** and the **Glory** were the same as described by Jesse Duplantis after his visit to **Heaven!**

> Exodus 24:12. *And the **LORD*** said to **Moses,** "Come up to **Me** on the mountain and be there, and I shall give you the tablets of stone, the **Torah (Teaching),** and the **commandments** which **I have written** so you can **teach** them." 13. And **Moses** and his minister **Joshua** rose up, and **Moses** went up on the **Mountain of God.** 14. And he said to the **elders,** "Wait here for us until we come back to you and, behold, **Aaron** and **Hur** are with you, if any man has any matters to do, let him come to them." 15. And **Moses** went up on the mountain and a cloud covered the mountain. 16. And the **Glory of the LORD*** stayed on **Mount Sinai** and the cloud covered it six days, and the seventh day He called to **Moses** out of the midst of the cloud. 17. And the sight of **the** <u>Glory of the LORD*</u> **was like a devouring fire on the top of the mountain in the** <u>eyes of the children of Israel</u>. 18. And **Moses** went into the midst of the cloud and went up on the mountain: and **Moses** was on the mountain **forty days** and **forty nights.***

Here again, all the **Children of Israel** saw the **Glory of God** and survived.

All believers who have the **Mark** of the **man** with the **Inkhorn** will be **Living** in the **Spirit Realm**, with everyone having **His Loving, Joyful Attributes** is going to keep each of us in ecstasy all the time!

THE RESURRECTED Y'SHUA

Matthew 28.1. *And after **Sabbaths**, on the First Day of the Week at dawn, **Miriam Magdalene** and the other **Miriam** came to see the tomb. 2. And behold there was a great earthquake: for there was an **angel** of the **Lord**, who descended from heaven, and after he came he rolled the stone away and was sitting upon it. 3. And his appearance was like lightning and his clothing **white as snow**. 4. And those who were **guarding** trembled from **fear** of **him** and became as dead. 5. And the **angel** said to the **women**, "You must not be afraid, for I know that you are seeking the crucified **Y'shua**: 6. He is not here, for **He** has risen just as **He** said. Come! See the place where **He** was laid. 7. And go quickly, you must tell **His disciples**, 'He has risen from the dead, and behold **He** is going before you into Galilee, for you will see **Him** there: behold I told you." 8. Then they left quickly from the tomb with fear and great joy, and were running to report to His disciples. 9. And behold **Y'shua** met the **women** saying, "Greetings." And they, who had approached Him, took hold of **His feet** and they **paid homage** to **Him**. 10. Then **Y'shua** said to them, "You must not be afraid: you must go, report to **My** brothers so they would go into Galilee, **they will see Me there**."*

In verse one, **Sabbaths** is a Hebrew idiom meaning that the plural can refer to every **weekly Sabbath** or a **Feast-day Sabbath**, which in this case was a **Feast-day, First Fruits of the Feast of Unleavened Bread**. In verse three, **White garments** represent being in a state of spiritual preparedness, from Ecclesiastes 9:8, *Let your **garments be always white**; and let your head lack no ointment.* Although in **Heaven** there will not be any woven garments, so cotton, wool, linen, or modern, man-made fabrics like nylon, acrylic, or polyester will **not** be there.

The Commissioning of the Disciples

Matthew 28:16. *And the eleven disciples went into Galilee to the mountain which **Y'shua** appointed to them, 17. and when they saw*

Him they paid homage to Him but they doubted. 18. Then when Y'shua came He spoke to them, saying, "All authority has been given to Me in heaven and upon the Earth. 19. Therefore when you go, you must now make disciples of all the heathens, 20. teaching them to keep all the things that I have been commanding you: (Amos 9:12) and behold I AM with you all the days until the end of the age."

In verse eighteen, **All Authority** includes over **Death,** Isaiah 25:8, Hosea 13:14, 1 Corinthians 15:54,55. We are ordered to make disciples of all Heathens throughout the world.

In **Matthew 28:19,** the Greek text contains a reference to Father, Son, and Holy Spirit. There is considerable evidence that this phrase was added at the Nicaean Council in **325 AD.** Several early Christian theologians who had seen the complete book of Matthew attested that the early copies of Matthew did not contain the phrase. Eusebius of Caesarea, who sat at the head table next to Constantine, was one of those, and even though he believed in the Trinity, he wrote that the phrase, "immersing in the name of the Father and of the Son and of the Holy Ghost" was not in the early texts. Today there are only two copies of Matthew earlier than the fourth century, and the last page of the Codex of each of those was destroyed many centuries ago. Eusebius also reported that Constantine insisted that the phrase "baptizing them in the name of the Father, Son, and Holy Spirit" be added to the Scripture, even over the objections of others.

The Resurrection of Y'shua

Mark 16.1. And, after the Sabbath passed, Miriam Magdalene and Miriam, mother of Jacob, and Salome bought spices so that when they came they could anoint Him. 2. And very early in the morning on the First Day of the Week, they came to the tomb as the sun was rising. 3. And they were saying among themselves, "Who will roll away the stone from the door of the tomb for us?" 4. And when they looked up they saw that the stone had been rolled away: for it was extremely large. 5. And after they entered the tomb they saw a young man sitting on the right side wearing a white robe, and they were distressed. 6. And he said to them, "Stop being distressed! You are seeking Y'shua *of Nazareth, the One Who was crucified: **He** is risen, **He** is not here: see the place where they put **Him**. 7. But you must now go, say to **His** disciples and to Peter, that 'He is to go before you into Galilee: you will see **Him** there just as **He** told you.'" 8. And after they went out they fled from the tomb, for they were quite beside themselves trembling with amazement: and they did not say anything: for they were afraid. This ends the Book of Mark.*

In verse one, the **Sabbath passed at sundown Saturday**. The **White Robe** represents being in a state of spiritual preparedness, from Ecclesiastes 9:8.

Miriam Magdalene, Miriam, mother of Jacob, and Salome bringing spices is unusual because women would never anoint a **man's** corpse, nor would men anoint a **woman's**. A body was prepared by washing, then anointing, then wrapping in linen, and finally placing the body in the tomb. A body was **never** removed from a tomb after two days for the **anointing**. John 19:38-40 says that **Nicodemus** brought **one hundred pounds of spices** when **he** and **Joseph** prepared the body, so there would have been no need even if the women could have anointed it. The one hundred Roman pounds of spices was an appropriate amount for royalty.

> John 19:38. *And after these things **Joseph**, the one from **Arimathea**, although, because of fear of the Jewish (leaders), he was a concealed disciple of **Y'shua**, asked Pilate if he could take the body of **Y'shua**: and Pilate did permit **him**. Therefore he came and took **His** body. 39. And **Nicodemus**, the one who came to **Him** on the earlier night, came too, bringing a mixture of **myrrh** and **aloe**, about a **hundred (Roman) pounds**. 40. Then they took the body of **Y'shua** and they bound it in linen cloth with the spices, as is a custom of the Jewish people to prepare for burial.*

One hundred Roman pounds is equivalent to about seventy-five English pounds, a great quantity used only for royalty. **His** body had to be prepared by men because a woman could not prepare a man's body nor a man prepare a woman's body.

> Luke 24:28. *Then they approached the village to which they were going (Emmaus), and **He** pretended to go farther on. 29. But they urged*

*Him saying, "You must now stay with us because it is toward evening and the day is already over." And **He** came in to stay with them. 30. And it happened while **He** reclined with them, when **He** took the bread He praised God and after He broke it **He** gave it to them, 31. and their eyes were opened and they recognized **Him**: then **He became invisible** for them. 32. And they said to one another, "Was not our heart burning in us as **He** was speaking to us on the way, as **He** was explaining the Scriptures to us?" 33. Then after they got up they returned to Jerusalem the same hour and found the eleven and those gathered with them, 34. saying that truly the Lord had risen and was seen by Simon. 35. And they were recounting the things (discussed by Y'shua) on the way and as He was recognized by them while He was breaking the bread.*

Y'shua, after **His** resurrection, reclined to eat with **Peter** and his wife, then became invisible, showing **He** could appear to be flesh and blood at one moment, then disappear in **His Spirit body** at will. Verse thirty-four identifies **Simon**, clarified by **Paul** in 1 Corinthians 15:5, as **Peter**, **not Simon** the **Zealot**, as one of the disciples walking with Him to **Emmaus**. Verse eighteen names **Cleopas** as the other disciple. While many people assume **Cleopas** is a man, the Greek spelling has a feminine genitive (possessive) ending, so many scholars speculate that this could have been **Peter's wife** on the road to **Emmaus** with him. On returning to Jerusalem, **Y'shua** joins all **eleven** disciples in an upper room.

His Appearance to the Disciples

Luke 24:36. *And while they were saying these things He stood in the midst of them and said to them, "Shalom Aleichem," ("Peace (be) with you.") 37. But becoming terrified and afraid they were thinking that they saw a spirit. 38. Then He said to them, "Why are you disturbed and why are the doubts going up in your heart? 39. You must now look at My hands and **My** feet because **I AM He**: you must **now touch Me** and see, because a **spirit does not have flesh and bone** just as you see **Me** having." 40. Then having said this **He** showed them **His hands and feet**. 41. But they still did not believe from the joy, and marveling **He** said to them, "Do you have something here to eat?" 42. And they gave **Him** a portion of **broiled fish**: 43. then after He took (it) **He ate in front of them**.*

Y'shua's body did rise in the **flesh**! But it was still **Spirit**!

> Luke 24:44. *And **He** said to them, "These (are) the messages I told you while I was still with you, that it is necessary for everything to be fulfilled that has been written about **Me** in the **Torah (Teaching) of Moses and in the Prophets and the Psalms**." 45. Then **He opened their minds and they understood the Scriptures**: 46. and **He** said to them that "Thus it has been written that the **Messiah** would suffer (Isaiah 53:5) and be raised from the dead on the third day, 47. and repentance would be preached in **His** name for forgiveness of sins for all the **heathens**. Beginning from Jerusalem 48. you (are) witnesses of these things. 49. Then behold, **I, Myself**, am sending **My Father's promise** upon you: but you must now stay in the city until you would be clothed in **power** from on high."*

Y'shua's Father's Promise is the **Immersion** (Baptism) of the **Holy Spirit**, given for the first time in Acts 2:1-12, from Joel 3:1. **Y'shua** opened the **minds** of the **Apostles** while **Elisha** opened their **eyes**, which is not a significant difference because both saw into the **Spiritual Realm** and our **minds** are a **hindrance** to understanding the **Spiritual**. We think too much, blocking our **Spiritual minds and eyes**.

The Appearance of Y'shua to the Disciples

> John 20:19. *Then when it was late on that day, on the **First Day of the Week**, and after the doors were shut where the **disciples** were because of fear of the Jewish leaders, **Y'shua** came and stood in their midst and said to them, **"Peace be with you." ("Shalom aleichem.")** 20. And after He said this He showed them His hands and His side. Then the disciples rejoiced, because they had seen the Lord. 21. Then **Y'shua** said to them again "Peace be with you: just as the Father sent Me, so **I am sending you**." 22. And after He said this He breathed upon them and said to them, "You must immediately **take** the Holy Spirit: 23. whomever you would **forgive**, their sins have been forgiven for them, whomever you would **retain** their sins have been **retained**."*

The **First Day of the week** is the Hebrew expression for **Sunday**, which begins at sundown on Saturday. **Y'shua's** Resurrected body has flesh that could be felt! Our Eternal Bodies will **not** have flesh. In Eternal Life, everything will be **Spirit**. In verse nineteen, the Disciples that were there were the ten, with **Thomas** the eleventh and Judas no longer with them. In this life, every believer is **Sent by God** to make more believers. Notice that **Y'shua** said to **Take the Holy Spirit**. Some translations say Receive the **Holy Spirit**, but the Greek text is clear that we are to **Take the Holy Spirit**. We are to eagerly seek the Immersion of the **Holy Spirit**. Every believer is also to recognize when someone repents to convert or has converted that it is proper to say to the repentant person, "Your sins are Forgiven."

Y'shua and Thomas

> John 20:24. *And **Thomas**, one of the twelve, called Twin, was not with them when **Y'shua** came. 25. Therefore the **other disciples** were telling him, "**We have seen the Lord.**" But he said to them, "Unless I could see the **mark of the nails in His hands and I could put my finger into the mark of the nails and I could put my hand into His side**, I will **not** believe." 26. And after **eight days His disciples** were again inside and **Thomas** (was) with them. After the doors were closed, **Y'shua** came and **He** was in the middle (of the room) and said, "**Peace to you.**" ("Shalom aleichem.") 27. Then He said to **Thomas**, "Put your finger here and see **My hands** and you must reach out your hand and you must put (it) into **My side**, and stop being faithless but (have) **faith.**" 28. **Thomas** answered and said to Him, "**My Lord and my God.**" 29. **Y'shua** said to him, "Because you have seen Me have you believed? **Blessed** (are) those who **have not seen and yet have believed**."*

It is easy to think that after **His** resurrection **Y'shua** was with the disciples continuously, but **He** was **not**. **Eight days** would have been a long time for them to go without seeing **His Resurrected Body.** Scripture cites a number of people resurrected from the dead, but only one of these, **Y'shua**, is resurrected to **eternal life. Elijah** and **Elisha** raised the **dead**, as did **Y'shua** on numerous occasions, then **Peter** raised **Tabitha** and **Paul** raised **Eutychus. All** of those who were raised simply **returned to their human, earthly, mortal bodies.** Since none is mentioned later in Scripture and apparently none is still alive, it is probably safe to believe that all have perished. Those resurrected bodies did not have any unusual qualities other than returning to life after being dead.

The Appearance of Y'shua to the Seven Disciples

John 21.1. *After these things* **Y'shua** *revealed Himself again to the disciples at the lake of Tiberias: and* **He** *revealed (Himself) like this. 2.* **Simon Peter** *and* **Thomas**, *the one called Twin, and* **Nathaniel**, *the one from Cana of Galilee, and the* **(sons) of Zebedee** *and* **two others** *of* **His disciples** *were together. 3.* **Simon Peter** *said to them, "I am going to fish* **(from now on)**." *They said to him, "We are coming and* **we (are) with you**." *They left and they embarked in the boat, and during that night they caught nothing. 4. And after dawn came* **Y'shua** *already stood on the shore, though the disciples did not yet know that it was* **Y'shua**. *5. Then* **Y'shua** *said to them, "Children, do you have any fish?" They answered Him, "No." 6. And* **He** *said to them, "You must cast the net to the right side of the boat, and you will find (fish)." Then they cast, and they no longer (had the) ability to haul (it) on account of the great number of the fish. 7. Then that disciple whom* **Y'shua** *loved said to* **Peter**, *"It is the* **Lord**." *Then after* **Simon Peter** *heard that it was the* **Lord** *he gird around his* **outer garment**, *for he was without his* **outer garment**, *and he threw himself into the lake, 8. but the other disciples came in the little boat, for they were not far off from the shore, only about* **two hundred cubits**, *dragging the net of fish. 9. Then as they got off on the shore they saw coals lying (there) with fish and bread being laid on (them). 10.* **Y'shua** *said to them, "You must now bring (some) of the fish which you just caught." 11. Then* **Simon Peter** *went up and hauled the net to the shore, full of a hundred fifty-three big fish: even when there were so many the net was not torn. 12.* **Y'shua** *said to them, "Come, you must eat breakfast." And not one of (the) disciples was bold enough to ask* **Him**, *"Who are You?" since they knew that it was the* **Lord**. *13.* **Y'shua** *came and took the bread and gave (it) to them, and likewise the roasted fish. 14. This (was) now (the)* **third time Y'shua** *was revealed to the disciples after* **He** *rose from (the) dead.*

In verse five, the Greek construction indicates **He** anticipates a negative answer to **His** question. **Peter's** outer garment was his **Prayer Shawl**, which was too bulky to wear for work. The **two hundred cubits** from shore equal three hundred yards.

Y'shua and Peter

> John 21:15. *Then while they ate breakfast* **Y'shua** *said to* **Simon Peter**, *"***Simon** *son of John, do you* **love Me** *more than these?" He said to* **Him**, *"Indeed* **Lord**, **You** *know that I* **love You**.*" He said to him, "You must continually feed* **My** *lambs." 16. Again* **He** *said to him a second time, "***Simon**, *son of John, do you* **love Me?***" He said to* **Him**, *"Indeed* **Lord**, **You** *have known that I* **love You**.*" He said to him, "You must continually* **tend My** *sheep." 17.* **He** *said to him the third time, "***Simon** *son of John, do you* **love Me?***" Peter became distressed because* **He** *said to him the third time, "Do you* **love Me?***" and he said to* **Him**, *"***Lord**, **You** *know all things,* **You** *know that I* **love You**.*"* **Y'shua** *said to him, "You must continually feed* **My** *sheep. 18. I most certainly say to you, when you were younger, you were girding yourself and you were walking where you wanted: but when you grow old, you will stretch your hands and another will clothe you and will carry (you) where you do not want (to go)." 19. And* **He** *said this indicating by what kind (of) death he will glorify God. And after* **He** *said this* **He** *said "You must continually follow* **Me**.*"*

In verse sixteen, **Tend** refers to the **ministry of the Good Shepherd, an instruction for everyone in ministry**. See "Son of David/Son of Joseph" in Glossary. In the question, "Do you **love Me**?" **Y'shua** and **Peter** use the archaic verb **Phileo,** and the more common verb **Agapao**, which many believe are different kinds of love. The Glossary article is given here:

Agapao is an ancient Greek verb used well over one hundred times in the New Testament. Many people believe that **agapao**, the verb form, and **agape**, a noun form, are strictly New Testament words. Both words were used in classic Greek. Its meaning in classic Greek was to welcome, entertain, and in relation to things, to be content. In first century Israel, the meaning was **love**, as in "**love your neighbor**" in Matthew 5:43. Other forms of **agapao** are: **agape**, a noun with both a **feminine form** and a **neuter form**, each meaning **love**; **agapemai**, a **noun indicating the object of love**; **agapenor**, meaning **loving manliness**, manly, used to refer to **heroes**; **agapesis**, a noun meaning **affection**; **agapetikos**, a noun meaning **affectionate**; and **agapetos**, an adjective meaning **worthy of love, beloved, esteemed**.

Of the above, only the verb **agapao**, the feminine noun **agape**, and the adjective **agapetos** are used in the Greek New Testament. The feminine noun **agape** uses case endings that are not used in any **classic Greek** literature. Case endings of Greek nouns and adjectives varied depending on how the word was used in the sentence. **Agape** apparently was in common usage by the **Hellenists** for several centuries before **Y'shua's** birth because it is used more than a dozen times in the Septuagint, the 250 BC Greek translation of the Hebrew Scriptures. At least four forms: the feminine **agape**, the neuter **agape**, **agapesis**, and **agapao**, are used in the Septuagint. The feminine **agape** is used in the Septuagint, in 2 Samuel 13:15, Song of Songs 2:4,5,7; 3:5,10; 5:8; 7:6; 8:4,6,7, and Ecclesiastes 9:1,6. Since the word **agape** is used by every New Testament author except Mark and is used about one hundred fifteen times in the New Testament, it must have been common throughout the Roman world. Koine Greek was the common language of the Roman Empire, not being replaced by Latin until the third and fourth centuries AD. The people spoke Greek in Rome, Corinth, Galatia, Ephesus, Philippi, Colossae, Thessalonika, and the various cities written to by the authors of Hebrews, Jacob, Peter, Jude, and John.

Phileo is a synonym of **agapao** but is used much less often in the New Testament. Some examples are: John 5:20. "..the **Father**, *God*, loves the **Son**, *Y'shua*;" John 11:3,30, where both verses speak of **Y'shua** loving Lazarus; John 16:27 speaks of the **Father loving** you and of you **loving Y'shua**, both verbs **Phileo**; and 1 Corinthians 16:22 "If someone does not love the **Lord**.."

In examining every use of both Agapao and Phileo, it is obvious that the words for **love** are **synonymous**.

Y'shua and the Beloved Disciple

> John 21:20. *Then **Peter** turned, (and) saw the disciple following (him), whom **Y'shua loved**, who also reclined **next to Him** at the supper and said, "**Lord**, who is the one who is giving **You** over?" 21. Therefore when **Peter** saw him he said to **Y'shua**, "**Lord**, what (about) him?" 22. **Y'shua** said to him, "If I want him to remain until I come, what (is it) to you? You must steadfastly follow **Me**." 23. Then this*

word came out among the brothers that that disciple would not die: but **Y'shua** *did not say to him that he would not die but, "If I want him to remain until I come, what (is it) to you?"*

In verse twenty, the verb is Agapao, and there is also a Hebrew idiom, "on the chest of," which means John was reclining next to **Y'shua**. The word Reclining in Glossary has:

Reclining to eat was the standard practice in first century Israel and was a symbol of **their being free**, not slaves, as in Egypt. At the Last Supper, as at every **Seder,** they **reclined,** and they even **reclined** at the **various meals** described in the Gospels. Sometimes there is no mention of the meal because when it was written that they **reclined**, the meal was understood. The couches they **reclined** on were angled at the table, so each only took up a small space at the table, not the full length of a couch or cushions. The person who **reclined** in front of someone was spoken of as **reclining** or **leaning on the bosom, or chest**, or, more commonly, the **lap of that person**, as John was at the **Last Seder**, John 13:23,25. To be in **Abraham's bosom** meant to have the **place of honor at a banquet**. Luke 16:23 tells of Lazarus in **Abraham's bosom**, referring to being a partaker of the same state of bliss as **Abraham in Paradise**.

The Resurrection of Messiah

1 Corinthians 15.1. *And I am making known to you, brothers, the Good News which I proclaimed to you, which then you accepted, in which you have also stood, 2. and through which you are being saved, if you hold fast to the kind of message I preached to you, except in case you believed in vain. 3. For I gave over to you at first what also I had accepted, that* **Messiah** *died on behalf of* **our sins** *according to the* **Scriptures** *4. and that* **He was buried** *and that* **He rose** *on the third day according to the* **Scriptures** *(Hos. 6:2) 5. and that* **He was seen by Cephas,** *then by the* **twelve:** *6. then He was seen by more than* **five hundred brothers** *at one time, most of whom are remaining until now, but some* **fell asleep:** *7. then He was seen by* **Jacob,** *then by all the* **apostles:** *8. and last of all as in an untimely birth* **He was seen by me.** *9. For I am the least of the* **apostles,** *who is not qualified to be called an* **apostle,** *because I persecuted the congregation of God: 10.*

but by (the) grace of God I am what I am, and His grace which is in me did not become ineffective, but I labored more than all of them, not I but the grace of God which is with me. 11. Now whether (it was) I or those, in this way we are proclaiming and so you believed.

Many seem to forget that **Y'shua** came to forgive sins, but that is what brings us into **ETERNAL LIFE.** The Scriptures to which Paul refers are the **Hebrew Text** that some disparage, calling them Old, as if out of date. **Cephas** is the Latin spelling of Peter's Hebrew name, **Kaf,** or Aramaic name, **Kefa.** Paul says some of the **five hundred** who saw **Y'shua** after His resurrection **fell asleep,** which is a Hebrew idiom for being dead. Paul is Humble about his being an **Apostle.** Paul's reference to **Y'shua** seeing the **Twelve Apostles** is sometime after Matthew was appointed, adding to the Eleven who witnessed His Ascension. (Acts 1:12)

The Resurrection of the Dead

1 Corinthians 15:12. *And if it is preached that **Messiah rose** from the **dead,** how are some among you saying that there is no **resurrection** of (the) **dead?** 13. But **if there is not a resurrection of (the) dead,** then **Messiah has not risen:** 14. and if **Messiah has not risen,** then also **our preaching (is) in vain,** and **your faith (is) in vain:** 15. and then we are being found **false witnesses of God, because we testified of God that He raised Messiah, Whom, if indeed the dead are not really being raised, He has not risen.** 16. For **if the dead are not raised, then Messiah has not been raised:** 17. and if **Messiah has not been raised, your faith is useless, you are still in your sins,** 18. and consequently those who **sleep in Messiah are lost.** 19. If we only have hope in **Messiah for this life, we are all miserable people.***

Paul makes a rational case for the **Resurrection** of the dead, which is the glorious future for all believers. **ETERNAL LIFE** is the goal for all of us and is mentioned in the New Testament about seventy-five times.

1 Corinthians 15:20. *But now **Messiah has been raised from (the) dead, First Fruits of those who have slept.** 21. For since death (is) through a man, then **resurrection** of (the) dead (is) through a Man.*

*22. For just as all are dying in Adam, so also will **all be made alive in Messiah**. 23. But each in his own order: **Messiah is First Fruits**, then those of the **Messiah at His coming**, 24. then the end, when He would give over the kingdom to **God and Father**, when every leader and every authority and every power will be brought to an end. 25. For it is necessary for Him to reign until the time when He would place all His enemies **under His feet**. 26. **Death** (is) the last enemy being abolished: 27. for **"He subjected all things under His feet."** (Psalm 8:7) and when He would say that all things have been subjected (it is) clear that the One who subjects all things to (Messiah is Himself) excepted. 28. But when all things would be subject to Him, then also the Son Himself would have been subjected to the One Who subjected all things to Him, so that God would be all in all.*

The Resurrection of **Y'shua**, as **First Fruits**, is proof that **all** believers will have ETERNAL LIFE. **Death** is the last enemy to be eradicated as all believers graduate to ETERNAL LIFE!

*1 Corinthians 15:29. Because what will **those who are immersed on behalf of the dead be doing?** If the **dead** are not **actually being raised**, then **why are they being immersed on their behalf?** 30. Why then are we in danger every hour? 31. I die daily, as surely as I may boast in you, brothers, in Messiah Y'shua our Lord. 32. If according to man I fought wild beasts in Ephesus, what (was) **the profit for me? If the dead are not raised**,*
"We should eat and we should drink,
for tomorrow we die." (Isa. 22:13)
33. You must stop being deceived:
"Evil associations are corrupting good customs." (Menander, Thais 218)
*34. **You must become righteously sober and stop sinning**, for some have ignorance of God, (and) I am speaking to arouse shame in you.*

The Righteous Dead are raised because, to be declared Righteous, they had to **stop sinning**.

The Resurrection Body

1 Corinthians 15:35. *But some will say, "How are the dead raised?"*
And "What sort of body is coming?" 36. Foolishness! **What you are**
sowing does not live unless it would die (first): *(John 12:24) 37.*
then what you are sowing, **you do not sow what will be the body**,
but a **naked seed**. *Perhaps it will turn out (to be) wheat or some of the*
other (grains): 38. but **God would give it a body just as He wished**,
and to each of the seeds its own body. 39. But not all flesh is the same,
but (there) is **one kind of flesh for people**, *and* **another kind of flesh**
for domestic animals, *and* **another flesh for birds**, *and* **another**
for fishes: *40. then (there are)* **heavenly bodies**, *and* **earthly bod-**
ies: another of the splendor of the heavenlies, *but* **another of the**
earthlies. *41. With* **another** *(kind of)* **splendor for (the) sun**, *and*
another *(kind of)* **splendor for (the) moon**, *and* **another splendor**
for (the) stars: *for* **star differs from star in splendor**.

Each body in the Hereafter will be a **Spirit Body**! That goes for each person,
each star, each of everything because everyone and everything in **Heaven**
will be **Spirit**, and **only Spirit**. There will be **No** Sun, **No** Moon.

1 Corinthians 15:42. *So also the* **resurrection of the dead**. *It is*
sown *in* **corruption**, *it is* **raised incorruptible**: *43. it is sown in*
dishonor, *it is raised in* **magnificence**: *it is sown in* **weakness**, *it is*
raised in **power**: *44. a body is sown* **fleshly**, *it is raised a* **spiritual**
body. *If there is a* **fleshly body**, *there is also a* **spiritual**. *45. And so it*
has been written, "The first man was Adam in living life," (Gen. 2:7)
the last Adam (has become) a life-giving spirit. 46. But the **spiritual**
was **not** *first but the* **physical**, *then the* **spiritual**. *47. The first man*
(is) from **dust** *of (the) earth, the second man out of* **Heaven**. *48. What*
sort of earthly (man), and such as these earthly (ones), and what sort
of the heavenly (One), then such as these **(born) of the heavenly na-**
ture: *49. and just as we* **bore constantly** *the* **image of the earthly**,
we will **bear constantly** *also the* **image of the heavenly One**.

Our **Earthly Bodies** were made from dust, being contaminated to start
with; then our **Spiritual Bodies** are from **Heaven**, **Pure** and **Holy**! So, in
ETERNAL LIFE, there will be no contamination, no sin! Our Spiritual

Bodies will bear the **Image of the Heavenly One**, the **LORD*** and **Y'shua, Who are ONE!** In **Heaven**, we finally get to be God-like!

> 1 Corinthians 15:50. *But I say this, brothers, that **flesh and blood are not able to inherit (the) Kingdom of God**, nor does corruption inherit incorruption. 51. Behold I am telling you a mystery: we will not all be **asleep (in death)**, but we will all be **transformed**, 52. in a moment, in a twinkling of an eye, at the last shofar: for a shofar will sound and the **dead will be raised incorruptible** and we **will be transformed**. (Isaiah 26:19, Daniel 12:13, Revelation 20:5) 53. For it is necessary to clothe this **corruptible (with the) incorruptible** and to **clothe** this mortal (with the) **immortal**. 54. And when this **mortal** will be **clothed immortal** and this **corruptible** will be clothed **incorruptible** then the written word will happen,*
>
> *"**Death was swallowed up in victory.**" (Isaiah 25:8)*
>
> *55. **Where, O Death, (is) your victory?***
>
> ***Where, O Death, (is) your sting?**" (Hosea 13:14)*
>
> *56. But **sin** (is) the **sting of death**, and the **power of sin** (is taken from) the **Torah** (Teaching): 57. but **thanks to God**, to the One Who gives us victory through our **Lord Y'shua Messiah**. 58. Thus, my beloved brothers, you must continually be steadfast, immovable, abounding in the work of the **Lord** always, since you have known that your labor is not without result in (the) **Lord**.*

Not one human cell will be in any body in Heaven! There will be no substance of any sort in Heaven! Paul makes a case for the Spirituality of Heaven! **Our bodies after the resurrection to eternal life** will be remarkably **different** from the bodies we now have. We should expect them to be like **Y'shua** was after His **resurrection**. What we know of Him and what is in Ezekiel 37:4 tell much about bodies resurrected to **eternal life**. Ezekiel 37:4 says: *And he said to me, "Prophesy **over these bones**, and say to them, O you **dry bones**, hear the word of the LORD*."* What we do **not** see in the English is that the phrase **"say to them"** does **not** refer to the **bones** but to the **people**. We know it refers to people because of the Hebrew word translated as "them." That word is masculine, while the word for bones is feminine, so that the LORD's* instruction to Ezekiel means (and is translated in this book) to a Jewish, Hebrew speaking reader *And*

He said to me, "Prophesy __over__, or in the direction of, these bones, and say to them, the people, O you dry bones, hear the word of the LORD*." The word translated __over__ can also be translated on, upon, above, or toward. Our Spiritual Bodies will not have bones, teeth, eyes, hair, hearts, or any other physical parts. Heaven, New Jerusalem, and everyone and everything there will be in **Spirit**, not physical in any way.

The Ascension of Y'shua

> Luke 24:50. *And He led them outside as far as Bethany, then as He raised His hands He blessed them. 51. And it happened while He was blessing them, He went away from them, and He was being brought up into the sky. 52. And after they paid homage to Him they returned to Jerusalem with great joy 53. and they were constantly in the Temple praising God.*

Luke also wrote the Book of Acts, citing His Ascension once more:

> Acts 1:6. *Therefore indeed those who came asked Him saying,* **"Lord, are You restoring the kingdom in Israel at this time?"** *7. But He said to them, "It is not for you to know (the) times or seasons which the Father set by His own authority, 8. but you will take power when the Holy Spirit comes upon you and you will be My witnesses in Jerusalem and in all Judea and Samaria and to (the) outermost (part) of the earth." 9. And after He said these things, as they were watching, He was lifted up and a cloud bore Him up and away from their eyes. 10. And as they were looking intently into the sky at His going, then there were two men in white clothing (who) stood by them, 11. and they said, "Men of Galilee, why have you stood looking into the sky? This* **Y'shua, Who, as He has been taken up from you into the sky, will come (back) in the same way as you saw Him going into the sky***."*

The Apostles were expecting the immediate beginning of His Messianic Reign! Many today are expecting the Messianic Reign Immediately! But this is not to be! The Reign will be in Heaven at the close of Judgment Day, with Judgment Day lasting a long time.

> Zechariah 14:4. *"And His (the LORD's) feet will stand in that Day upon the Mount of Olives, which is before Jerusalem on the east, and*

the Mount of Olives will split in the middle toward the east and toward the west and there will be a very great valley, and half of the mountain will remove toward the north and half of it toward the south."

That split of the Earth will not be Physical but will be Spiritual, as His reign with the LORD* will be Spiritual. In Heaven, everyone and everything will be Spiritual. See the last chapter of *Glimpses into the Spiritual Realm*, which explains that in detail.

5

TRAVEL IN THE SPIRIT REALM

There, in Heaven, will be **no** cars, bikes, planes, or trains; **no** physical means of travel; **no** roads either.

> Genesis 18.1. **And the LORD* appeared** to him in the plains of *Mamre and **he, Abraham, was sitting in the tent door** in the heat of the day. 2. And **he lifted up his eyes and looked, and there were three men standing by him**. And when he saw them, he ran from the tent door to meet them and he bowed toward the ground 3. and said, "My **Lord**, if now I have found favor in Your sight, do not pass by, I pray **You**, from **Your** servant: 4. let a little water, I pray you, be brought and wash your feet and rest yourselves under the tree. 5. And I shall get a morsel of bread and comfort your hearts for you. After that you will pass on, for that is why you have come to your servant." And they said, "So do as you have said." 6. And Abraham hastened into the tent to Sarah and said, "**Make ready quickly three measures** of fine meal, knead it and make cakes." 7. And Abraham ran to the herd and fetched a good, tender calf and gave it to a young man and he hastened to dress it. 8. And he took butter, milk, and the calf which he had dressed and set it before them, and he stood by them under the tree and they ate.*

Abraham was sitting by his tent when suddenly, three men stood beside him. They were two spirit beings plus the **LORD***. In verse three, the pronouns **You** and **Your** are singular, recognizing the presence of God; in verse four, they are plurally lowercase, because the angels are included. **Three measures, seahs**, are about **twenty-one quarts**, enough bread for many.

Genesis 18:9. *And they said to him, "Where is Sarah your wife?" And he said, "There – in the tent." 10. And **He** said, "I shall certainly return to you at this time next year and, see, Sarah your wife will have a son." (Rom. 9:9) And Sarah listened in the tent door, which was behind him. 11. Now Abraham and Sarah were old and well up in age: the manner of women had ceased to be with Sarah. 12. Therefore Sarah laughed within herself saying, "After I have grown old will I have pleasure, my lord being old also?" 13. And the **LORD*** said to Abraham, "Why did Sarah laugh saying, 'Will I, who am old, a surety bear a child?' 14. Is anything too hard for the **LORD***? (Jer. 32:17, Matt. 19:26, Luke 1:37) At the time appointed I shall return to you, about this time next year, and Sarah will have a son." (Rom. 9:9) 15. Then Sarah denied it saying, "I did not laugh," for she was afraid. And He said, "No, but you did laugh."*

In the **Spirit Realm**, like Genesis 18, Moves will be by the **Spirit**, by thought, as with Ezekiel when he appeared to the elders in Tel Aviv, Babylon, yet saw the conditions in Judah. The **Living Creatures** of Ezekiel are **Spiritual** creatures, not **physical**, so they carry Ezekiel in the **Spirit** to **Jerusalem**. This is **Tel Aviv, Babylon**, which existed roughly 2,300 years before the founding of **Tel Aviv, Israel**.

The Spirit Takes Ezekiel Up and carries him in the Spirit to Babylon!

Ezekiel 3:12. *Then the **Spirit took me up** and I heard behind me a great rushing, a voice saying, Blessed be the **Glory of the LORD*** from His place. 13. I also heard the noise of the wings of the **living creatures** that touched one another and the noise of the wheels over against them and a noise of a great rushing. 14. So the **Spirit lifted me up and took me away** and I went in bitterness, in the heat of my spirit, but the hand of the **LORD*** was strong upon me. 15. Then I came to those of the **captivity** at **Tel Aviv** (Babylon), who lived by the **river of Chebar** and I sat where they sat and remained there dumbfounded among them seven days.*

Ezekiel was later carried by the Babylonians to Babylon.

Visions for Jerusalem, given to Ezekiel in Babylon by the River Chebar:

> Ezekiel 8.1. *And it happened in the sixth year, in the sixth month, on the fifth day of the month, as I sat in* **my house and the elders of Judah sat before me**, *that the hand of* **Adonai**, *the* **LORD***, *fell upon me there. 2. Then I beheld and, lo, a likeness as the appearance of fire. From the appearance of his loins even downward, fire, and from his loins even upward, as the appearance of brightness, as the color of amber. 3. And he put forth the form of a hand and took me by a lock of my head, and the* **spirit lifted me up between the earth and the heavens** *and brought me in the* **visions of God for Jerusalem**, *to the door of the inner gate that looks toward the north where the seat of the image of* **jealousy** *was, which provokes to* **jealousy**. *4. And behold, the* **glory of the God of Israel** *was there, according to the vision that I saw in the valley.*

The **Jealousy** was the **LORD***'s because of the **Desecration of the Sanctuary!**

Then Ezekiel sees, in the Spirit, the evil being done there.

> Ezekiel 8:5. *He said to me, Son of man,* **lift up your eyes now toward the way of the north**. *So I lifted up my eyes the way toward the north, and behold, northward at the gate of the altar this image of* **jealousy** *was in the entry. 6. He said furthermore to me, Son of man,* **do you see what they are doing**? *The* **great abominations** *that the* **House of Israel commits here**, *that I should go* **far off from My Sanctuary**? *But you will see again still* **greater abominations**.

Ezekiel sees what is going on in Jerusalem at the Sanctuary while Ezekiel's physical body is still in Babylon.

> Ezekiel 8:7. *Then He brought me to the door of the court and when I looked, behold a hole in the wall. 8. Then He said to me, Son of man, now* **dig in the wall**. *And when* **I had dug in the wall**, *there was a* **door**. *9. And He said to me, Go in and observe the wicked* **abominations** *that they are* **doing here**. *10. So I went in and saw, and behold* **every form of creeping things, and abominable beasts, and all**

*the idols of the House of Israel, portrayed all around on the wall. 11. And **seventy men of the elders of the House of Israel** stood before them, and in the midst of them stood Jaazaniah the son of Shafan, every man with his fire-pan in his hand, and a thick cloud of incense went up. 12. Then He said to me, Son of man, have you seen what the old men of the House of Israel do in the dark, each man in the chambers of his imagery? For **they say, the LORD* does not see us. The LORD* has forsaken the earth**. 13. He also said to me, **Turn** yet again, you will see **greater abominations that they do**. 14. Then He brought me to the door of the gate of the LORD's* House which is toward the north and, behold, there sat **women weeping for Tammuz**.*

In verse fourteen, **Tammuz** was one of three things: the **youthful husband, son, or lover of Ishtar,** the fertility goddess of Babylon, called Ashtoret in Canaan. Worship of **Tammuz** lasted well into the Middle Ages.

Ezekiel 8:15. *Then He said to me, Have you seen this, O son of man? Turn yet again, you will see **greater abominations** than these. 16. And He brought me into the **inner court of the LORD's* House** and, behold, at the door of the **Temple** of the LORD*, between the **porch and the altar, were about twenty-five men with their backs toward the Temple of the LORD***, and their faces toward the east and they **worshipped the sun** toward the east. 17. Then He said to me, Have you seen this, O son of man? Is it a light thing to the **House of Judah** that they commit the **abominations** which they **commit here**? For they have filled the land with **violence** and have **returned to provoke Me to anger** and, lo, they put the **branch to their nose**. 18. Therefore **I will also deal in fury**. My eye will **not spare, neither will I have pity** and though they cry in My ears with a loud voice, yet **I will not hear** them.*

In verse sixteen, **Temple** refers to the **Sanctuary** because the **inner court is in the Temple,** so this is **between the altar and the Sanctuary**. We do not know what is being done to anger God so much, but it has to be some obscure idolatrous rite. All this is shown to Ezekiel in the Spirit while his physical body is in Tel Aviv, Babylon

Angels Show us the Means of Travel:

Judges 6:11. *And an **angel of the LORD*** came and sat under an oak which was in Afrah that belonged to Joash the Abiezrite, and his son **Gideon** threshed wheat by the wine press, to hide it from the Midianites. 12. And the **angel of the LORD*** appeared to him and said to him, the **LORD*** is with you, you mighty man of valor.*

This **Angel** just appeared and was actually the **LORD* Himself!**

Judges 6:13. *And **Gideon** said to him, Oh my lord, if the **LORD*** is with us, why then has all this befallen us? And where are all His miracles which our fathers told us about, saying, Did not the **LORD*** bring us up from Egypt? But now the **LORD*** has forsaken us and delivered us into the hands of the Midianites. 14. And the **LORD*** looked at him and said, <u>Go in this your might</u> and **you will save Israel** from the hand of Midian! Have I not sent you?*

So, the LORD* Himself says, "<u>Go in this your might</u>," and tells Gideon he will save Israel, which Gideon does with only 300 unarmed men against more than 120,000 armed Midianites, some accomplishment for a man who had been hiding from the Midianites.

Judges 6:15. *And he said to **Him**, Oh my Lord, With what will I save Israel? See, my family is poor in Manasseh and I am the least in my father's house.*

Gideon made excuses as Moses had done before him.

Judges 6:16. *And the **LORD*** said to him, Surely I shall be with you and you will strike Midian as one man.*

Gideon, still hesitant, asks for a sign.

Judges 6:17. *And he said to **Him**, If now I have found favor in Your sight, then **show me a sign** that You are talking with me. 18. Now, please! Do not leave from here until I come to **You** and bring forth my offering and set it before **You**.*

99

*And **He** said, **I AM** staying until you come again. 19. And **Gideon** went in and made ready a kid and **unleavened** cakes of an **ephah** of flour. He put the flesh in a basket and he put the broth in a pot and brought it out to Him under the oak, and presented it.*

In verse eighteen, the Great Anokhi, the **I AM**, is the visitor to Gideon, and in verse nineteen, Gideon prepares a great feast for the **LORD*** with an **Ephah, 60% of a bushel** of wheat.

Fire From Heaven

Judges 6:20. *And the **angel of God** said to him, Take the flesh and the unleavened cakes and lay them upon this rock and pour out the broth. And he did so. 21. Then the **angel of the LORD*** put forth the end of the staff that was in his hand and touched the flesh and the unleavened cakes and there rose up **fire out of the rock**, and consumed the flesh and the unleavened cakes. Then the **angel of the LORD*** departed from his sight.*

No wonder the **Angel** was named **Miracle**. Earlier, two **Angels** had come to Lot in Sodom:

Gideon then goes on to defeat and over-run the Midianites with just 300 unarmed men, chasing them completely out of Israel!

Another Angel Appears

Judges 13:2. *And there was a certain man of Zarah of the family of the Danites, whose name was Manoah, and his wife was barren and had not borne. 3. And an **angel** of the LORD* appeared to the woman and said to her, Behold now, you are barren and have not borne, but you will conceive and bear a son. 4. Now therefore beware, I pray you, and, **Do not drink wine or strong drink!** and **Do not eat any unclean thing!** 5. for, behold, you will conceive and bear a son and no razor will come on his head, for the child will be a **Nazirite** to God from the womb, and he will begin to deliver Israel out of the hand of the Philistines. 6. And the woman came and told her husband saying, **A man of God** came to me and his countenance was like the countenance of* *an **angel** of God, very awesome, but I did not ask him where he was from, neither did he tell me his name. 7. But he said to me, Behold, you will conceive and bear a son and now, **Do not drink wine or strong drink! Do not eat any unclean thing!** for the child will be a **Nazirite** to God from the womb to the day of his death.*

The son to be born will be a **Nazirite**! **Nazirite** is not in any way related to **Nazareth**, which in Hebrew is **Natsrat**, where **Y'shua** grew up.

Judges 13:8. *Then **Manoah** entreated the **LORD*** and said, O my **Lord**, let the man of God whom you sent come to us again and teach us what we will do with the child that will be born. 9. And **God** heard the voice of **Manoah** and the **angel** of God came to the woman again as she sat in the field, but **Manoah** her husband was not with her. 10. And the woman made haste and ran and told her **husband** and said to him, Behold, the man who came to me that day has appeared to me.*

11. And Manoah got up and went after his wife and came to the man and said to him, Are you the man who spoke to my wife?

And he said I am.

*12. And **Manoah** said, Now let your words come to pass. What will be done with the **child** and his **work**?*

*13. And the **angel** of the **LORD*** said to **Manoah**, Of all that I said to the woman let her beware. 14. She may not eat of anything that comes from the vine. **She will not drink wine or strong drink! She will not eat any unclean thing! She will observe all that I commanded her!** 15. And **Manoah** said to the **angel** of the LORD*, I pray you, let us detain you until we make ready a kid for you.*

Angel Ascends in the Flame

Judges 13:16. *And the **angel** of the **LORD*** said to **Manoah**, Though you detain me, I shall not eat of your bread and if you will offer a burnt offering, you must offer it to the **LORD***. For **Manoah** did not know that he was an **angel** of the **LORD***. 17. And **Manoah** said to the **angel** of the **LORD***, What is your name, so when your sayings come to pass we can honor you? 18. And the **angel** of the **LORD*** said to him, Why do you ask this about my name, seeing it is **Miracle**? 19. So*

*Manoah took a kid with a grain offering and offered it to the **LORD***
*on a rock, and (the **angel**) did **wondrously**, and **Manoah** and his*
wife looked on. 20. For it happened when the flame went up toward
*heaven from the altar, that the **angel** of the **LORD*** ascended in the*
*flame of the altar. And **Manoah** and his wife looked at it and fell to*
the ground on their faces.

The Hebrew **Peli** means Wonderful, Miraculous, Amazing, Marvelous,
Astounding.

Two Angels come to Lot

Genesis 19.1. *And **two angels came** to Sodom in the evening and*
***Lot** was sitting in the gate of Sodom. And when **Lot** saw them he*
rose up to meet them and he bowed himself with his face toward the
ground. 2. And he said, "Behold now, my lords, turn in, I pray you,
into your servant's house and tarry all night and wash your feet and you
*will rise up early and go on your way." And they said, "No. But **we will***
***stay in the street** all night." 3. And he pressed upon them greatly and*
*they went in with him and **entered his house** and he made a **feast** for*
*them and baked **unleavened bread** and they ate.*

TEMPORARY SPIRIT BODIES

6

The **Living God** has transformed **physical bodies** into **Spirit Bodies** to save **His Saints**. **Jonah** was transformed into his **Spirit body,** so there was no way he could drown, nor was there any way the whale could **digest his Spirit**. **Not** being **physical** has definite advantages in **unreal** situations. The **LORD*** can transform anyone from **physical** to **Spirit** at His whim, then back to **physical** just as quickly and just as easily; **nothing is too difficult for Him**.

> Jonah 2:1. *Now the **LORD*** had prepared a great fish to swallow **Jonah**. And **Jonah** was in the belly of the fish three days and three nights. 2. Then **Jonah prayed** to the LORD* his God out of the fish's belly 3. and said, I cried for myself to the LORD* by reason of my affliction and **He answered me**. Out of the inmost of the grave I cried and **You** heard my voice. 4. For **You** had thrown me into the deep, in the midst of the seas and the floods compassed me about. All Your billows and **Your** waves passed over me. 5. Then I said, I am cast out of **Your** sight, yet I shall look again toward **Your** holy Temple. 6. The waters surrounded me, even to my very life. The depth closed all around me, the reeds were wrapped about my head. 7. I went down to the bottom of the mountains. The earth with her **bars** was about me forever, yet You have brought up my life from corruption, **LORD*** my God. 8. When my life fainted within me I remembered the **LORD*** and my **prayer** came in to **You** in **Your holy Temple**. 9. Those who observe **lying vanities** forsake their own loving kindness. 10. But I shall sacrifice to **You** with the voice of thanksgiving. I shall pay that which I have vowed. **Salvation** is of the **LORD***.*

Jonah prayed while in his **Spirit** body, showing that a **Spirit** does not need **physical vocal cords** to communicate. The **Bars** are the gates of **Hell**, the **Underworld** that could not detain **Jonah**. When the whale spit **Jonah** onto the beach, he was **instantly transformed** into his **physical body**. **Lying vanities** are worthless, vain things.

The Spirit Body can endure super high temperatures;

The **Spirit body, not** having **flesh,** can endure **high temperatures** and **other physical challenges**, so the three Hebrews thrown into the fiery furnace had **no problem** from the **flames** and the **heat**. Their **prayer shawls** were **Spirit,** as well as their **bodies** were **Spirit,** so **no** odor of smoke stuck to them. Immediately after leaving the furnace, **they returned to their physical bodies** with their **physical prayer shawls, but no odor of smoke came with them**.

> Daniel 3:1. *Nebuchadnezzar the king made an **image of gold**, whose height was sixty cubits, its breadth six cubits: he set it up in the plain of Dura, in the province of **Babylon**. 2. Then **Nebuchadnezzar** the king sent to gather together the satraps, the governors, and the captains, the judges, the treasurers, the counsellors, the magistrates, and all the rulers of the provinces to come to the dedication of the image which **Nebuchadnezzar** the king had set up. 3. Then the satraps, the governors and captains, the judges, the treasurers, the counsellors, the magistrates, and all the rulers of the provinces were gathered together for the dedication of the image that **Nebuchadnezzar** the king had set up, and they stood before the **image** that **Nebuchadnezzar** had set up. 4. Then a herald cried aloud,*
>
> *To you it is commanded, O peoples, nations, and languages, 5. at what time you hear the sound of the horn, flute, harp, sambuke, psaltery, pipe, and all kinds of music, fall down and worship the golden image that **Nebuchadnezzar** the king has set up, 6. and whoever does not fall down and worship will the same hour be cast into the midst of a **burning fiery furnace**. (Rev. 13:15)*

That furnace was at least ninety feet high, equivalent to a nine-story building. Archeologists have found remnants of such furnaces.

Daniel 3:7. Therefore at that time, when all the peoples heard the sound of the horn, flute, harp, sambuke, psaltery, and all kinds of music, **all the peoples***, the nations, and the languages fell down and* **worshipped** *the golden* **image** *that* **Nebuchadnezzar** *the king had set up.*

Nebuchadnezzar ruled one hundred twenty provinces, with the population of each province ordered to respond to the **call** to **Worship** the **Image Nebuchadnezzar** had set up.

Daniel 3:8. Therefore at that time certain Chaldeans came near and accused the **Jews***. 9. They spoke and said to king* **Nebuchadnezzar***, O king, live forever. 10. You, O king, have made a decree that every man who* **hears** *the sound of the* **horn, flute, zither, sambuke, harp,** *and* **double-pipe***, and all kinds of music will* **fall down** *and* **worship** *the* **golden image***. 11. And whoever does not fall down and* **worship** *should be cast into the midst of a* **burning fiery furnace***. 12. There are certain* **Jews** *whom you have set over the affairs of the province of Babylon;* **Shadrach, Meshach,** *and* **Abednego***. These men, O king, have* **not paid attention to you***: they do not* **serve your gods** *or* **worship the golden image** *which you have set up.*

Shadrach, Meshach, and **Abednego** were singled out as being disobedient, even though they held high positions in **Nebuchadnezzar's** government; in **not worshipping** the **Image** when they **heard** the music, they were visibly rebellious.

Daniel 3:13. Then **Nebuchadnezzar** *in rage and fury commanded to bring* **Shadrach, Meshach,** *and* **Abednego***. Then they brought these men before the king. 14.* **Nebuchadnezzar** *spoke and said to them, Is it true, O* **Shadrach, Meshach***, and* **Abednego***, that you do* **not serve my gods** *or* **worship the golden image** *which I have set up? 15. Now if you are ready that at what time you hear the sound of the* **horn, flute, harp, sambuke, psaltery,** *and* **double pipe***, and* **all kinds** *of music, you fall down and worship the image which I have made, well, but* **if you do not worship, you will be cast the same hour into the midst of a burning fiery furnace***, and who is the* **God** *that will* **deliver you** *out of my hands?*

The three Jews have a ready answer for **Nebuchadnezzar!**

> Daniel 3:16. ***Shadrach, Meshach,*** *and **Abednego** answered and said to king **Nebuchadnezzar**, we have no need to answer you in this matter. 17. Behold, **our God Whom we serve is able to deliver us from the burning fiery furnace** and He will deliver us out of your hand, O king. 18. But if not, be it known to you, O king, that* <u>**we will not serve your gods or worship the golden image**</u> *which you have set up.*

The Jews say, "OK, our God will take care of us!"

> Daniel 3:19. *Then **Nebuchadnezzar** was full of fury and the form of his visage was changed against **Shadrach, Meshach,** and **Abednego**; therefore he spoke and commanded that they should **heat the furnace seven times more than it would normally be heated**. 20. And he commanded the mightiest men that were in his army to bind **Shadrach, Meshach,** and **Abednego**, and to cast them into the **burning fiery furnace**. 21. Then these men were bound in their **cloaks**, their tunics, their turbans, and their other garments, and were cast into the midst of the burning fiery furnace. 22. Therefore because the king's commandment was urgent and the furnace exceedingly hot, the **flame of the fire slew those men who took up Shadrach, Meshach, and Abednego**. 23. And these three men, **Shadrach, Meshach,** and **Abednego**, fell down bound into the midst of the **burning fiery furnace**.*

Their **cloaks** were their **Prayer Shawls;** Now God had transformed them and all their garments into **Spirit form**, so the heat had no effect on them, **none at all**!

> Daniel 3:24. *Then **Nebuchadnezzar** the king was alarmed and stood up in haste, spoke and said to his counsellors, **Did we not cast three men bound into the midst of the fire?** They answered and said to the king, **True**, O king.*

Who is this **fourth** man?

> Daniel 3:25. *He answered and said, Lo, **I see four men loose, walking** in the midst of the fire and they have no hurt! And the form of the fourth is like a **Son of God**.*

God not only transformed the three Jews into the Spirit Realm, but **He** gave them a **Comforter** to walk with them in the flames.

> Daniel 3:26. *Then Nebuchadnezzar came near to the door of the burning fiery furnace and spoke, and said, **Shadrach, Meshach,** and **Abednego**, you **servants of the Most High God**, come forth, and come here. Then **Shadrach, Meshach**, and **Abednego**, came out of the **midst of the fire**. 27. The satraps, governors and captains and the king's counsellors, being gathered together, saw these men, upon whose **bodies** the **fire** had **No** power, **nor** was the **hair** of their head **singed, neither** were their **cloaks changed, nor** the smell of **fire** had passed on them. 28. **Nebuchadnezzar** spoke and said, **Blessed be the God of Shadrach, Meshach, and Abednego**, Who has sent **His angel** and **delivered His servants** who **trusted in Him** and have changed the king's word and yielded their bodies, so **they could not serve or worship any god except their own God**. 29. Therefore I make a decree, That every **people, nation,** and **language** that speaks anything amiss **against the God of Shadrack, Meshach, and Abednego**, will be cut in pieces and their houses will be made a dunghill because there is **no other God that can deliver after this sort.***

Nebuchadnezzar saw firsthand and knew the **power** of the only **Living God** but still did not yield his heart to the LORD*. **Nebuchadnezzar** is then conquered by **Darius,** who issues a decree similar to one issued by **Nebuchadnezzar.** This decree brings **Daniel** into jeopardy, so it is **Daniel's** turn to be transformed into his **Spirit body**!

> Daniel 6:1. *And **Darius** the Mede took the kingdom, being about sixty-two years old. 2. It pleased **Darius** to set over the kingdom a hundred twenty satraps, who should be over the whole kingdom 3. and over these, **three presidents**, of whom **Daniel** was one, so the satraps would give accounts to them, and the king should have no loss. 4. Then this **Daniel** was preferred above the presidents and satraps, because an excellent spirit was in him, and the king thought to set him over the whole realm.*

Then worldly jealousy kicks in:

> Daniel 6:5. *Then the **presidents and satraps** sought to find occasion against **Daniel** concerning the kingdom, but they could find no occasion or fault, forasmuch as he was faithful: neither was there any error or fault found in him. 6. Then these men said, We will not find any occasion against this **Daniel**, unless we find it against him concerning the **law of his God**. 7. Then these **presidents and satraps** assembled together to the king and said thus to him, King **Darius**, live forever! 8. All the **presidents** of the kingdom, the **governors**, the **satraps**, the **counsellors**, and the **captains** have consulted together to establish a royal statute and to make a firm interdict, that whoever will **ask a petition** of any **god** or **man** for thirty days, save of you, O king, he will be cast into the **den of lions**. 9. Now, O king, establish the interdict and sign the writing, so it cannot be changed, according to the law of the Medes and Persians, which does not change. 10. Therefore king **Darius** signed the writing and the interdict.*

The cycle repeats! Daniel does **not** deny his **Faith,** brazenly **not** hiding his prayer to the Living God!

> Daniel 6:11. *Now when **Daniel** knew that the writing was signed, he went into his house, his windows being open in his chamber toward Jerusalem, he kneeled upon his knees three times a day and **prayed** and **gave thanks** before his God, as he had before. 12. Then these men assembled and found **Daniel praying** and making **supplication** before his God. 13. Then they came near and spoke before the king concerning the king's interdict, Have you not signed an interdict that every man **who will ask a petition of any god or man** within thirty days, save of you, O king, will be cast into the **den of lions**?*
>
> *The king answered and said, The thing is true, according to the law of the Medes and Persians, which cannot be changed.*

The entire ruling **establishment** gathered against **Daniel**, leaving the king **no** alternative, but to sentence **Daniel** to be cast into the lions' den.

> Daniel 6:14. *Then they answered and said before the king, That **Daniel**, who is of the children of the captivity of **Judah**, does not regard*

*you, O king, or the interdict that you have signed, but makes his **petition three times a day**.*

Daniel 6:15. *Then the king, when he heard these words, was sore displeased with himself, and set his heart on **Daniel** to deliver him and he labored till the going down of the sun to deliver him. 16. Then these men assembled to the king and said to the king, Know, O king, that the law of the Medes and Persians is, That **no interdict** or **statute** which the king establishes **may be changed**. 17. Then the king commanded, and they brought **Daniel** and cast him into the **den of lions**. Now the king spoke and said to **Daniel**, Your **God, Whom you serve continually, will Himself deliver you**. 18. And a stone was brought and laid upon the mouth of the den and the king sealed it with his own signet, and with the signet of his lords, so the purpose could not be changed concerning **Daniel**.*

The king speaks out, saying that **Daniel's** God would deliver him. Then **Daniel's** physical body was thrown into the lions' den, and he was immediately transformed into his **Spirit** body! The lions could not in any way harm the **Spirit** because they are only **physical** and **Daniel's** body had **no** flesh, **no** physical attributes at all, so they ignored the **Spirit**, which the lions could **Not** see, smell, or hear.

Daniel 6:19. *Then the king went to his palace, and passed the night fasting, neither were instruments of music brought before him and his sleep went from him. 20. Then the king rose very early in the morning and went in haste to the **den of lions**. 21. And when he came to the den, he cried with a lamentable voice to **Daniel**: the king spoke and said to **Daniel**, O **Daniel, servant of the Living God**, is your **God**, Whom you serve continually, able to **deliver you** from the lions?*

The name Daniel means God is my Judge. Daniel, too, is immediately transformed into his Spirit body!

Daniel 6:22. *Then **Daniel** said to the king, O king, live forever! 23. **My God has sent His angel** and has shut the lions' mouths, so they have not hurt me: forasmuch as innocence was found in me before Him and also before you, O king, I have done no hurt. 24. Then the* *king was exceeding glad for him and commanded that they should take* **Daniel** *up out of the den. So* **Daniel** *was taken up out of the den and no manner of hurt was found on him, because he believed in his God. 25. And the king commanded and they brought those men who had accused* **Daniel** *and they cast them into the den of lions, them, their children and their wives, and the lions had the mastery of them, and broke all their bones in pieces before they came to the bottom of the den.*

Being in the **Spirit** kept **Daniel** from even tempting the lions to attack him. Animals can, at times, see into the **Spirit Realm,** as testified in the book *Angels on Assignment* by Pastor Roland Buck. On being lifted out of the lion's den, Daniel is immediately transformed into his physical body.

Philip and Ezekiel are translated in the **Spirit** to travel miles, immediately being transformed into their physical bodies on arrival.

Philip and the Cushite Eunuch

Acts 8:26. *Then an* **angel** *of the* **Lord** *spoke to* **Philip** *saying, "Rise and* **go down south** *on the road that* **descends** *from* **Jerusalem** *to* **Gaza.***" This is wilderness. 27. And when he got up he went. And there was a man, an* **Ethiopian eunuch***, of great authority under Candace queen of the Ethiopians, who was over all her royal treasury, who had come in order to* **worship** *in* **Jerusalem** *28. and was returning. And while he was sitting in his* **chariot** *he was reading the prophet* **Isaiah***. 29. And the* **Spirit** *said to* **Philip***, "You must approach and join this one in the chariot." 30. And as he was running up* **Philip** *heard him reading* **Isaiah** *the prophet and said, "Do you really* **understand** *what you are reading?" 31. And he said, "How indeed would I be able unless* **someone** *would guide me?" He urged* **Philip** *to come up to sit with him. 32. And the portion of the Scripture which he was reading was this:*

"As a sheep was led to **slaughter***

and as a **lamb** *before the one* **shearing** *it (is) mute,*

in the same way He does not open His mouth.

33. In **His** *humiliation* **His justice** *was taken away:*

who will describe His generation?

because His life is taken from the earth." (Isa. 53:7,8)

An **Angel** comes to **Philip**, telling him to go down to the road to **Gaza,** where **Philip** will meet the Ethiopian Secretary of the Treasury of the queen, **Candace**. The **Officer** of Candace had come to Jerusalem to celebrate **Passover** and was on his way home after the Feast of Unleavened Bread was over. **Philip** overheard the officer reading from the Book of Isaiah, questioning him about the passage he was reading; then, the officer invited **Philip** to join him so **Philip** could explain the passage.

> Acts 8:34. *And the **eunuch** said to **Philip**, "I beg you, concerning whom is the prophet saying this? Concerning himself or concerning some other?" 35. And **Philip** then opened his mouth and having begun from this **Scripture** he proclaimed to him the **Good News** (about) **Y'shua**. 36. And as they were going along the way, they came upon some water, and the **eunuch** said, "Look! **Water**! What prevents me from being **immersed**?", 38. And he ordered the chariot to stop and **Philip** and the **eunuch** both went down into the water, and he **immersed** him. 39. And when they came up **out** of the **water**, (the) **Spirit of the Lord** took **Philip** away and the **eunuch** no longer saw him, then (the **eunuch**) went on his way rejoicing. 40. And **Philip** was found in **Ashdod**: and he was evangelizing, coming through all the cities until he came into **Caesarea**.*

Philip explained how that related to **Y'shua**; then, the officer immediately wanted to be immersed in nearby water. This immersion was unusual because immersion was normally private, individual, but this time **Philip** immersed him, wading into the water and putting his hand on the eunuch's head, then holding him down to force him to struggle, symbolizing the struggle of a newborn baby to be born. **Ashdod** is the Hebrew name of the city; some translations use the Greek name, Azotus. In this passage, **Philip** is transformed into his **Spirit**, then back into his **Physical** body once he arrived in **Ashdod**.

About six hundred years before **Philip**, **Ezekiel** had a similar transformation.

> Ezekiel 2.1. *And He said to me, Son of man, stand upon your feet and I shall speak to you. 2. And the **Spirit entered me** when He spoke to me and set me upon my feet, so I heard **Him** Who spoke to me. 3. And He said to me, Son of man, I am sending you to the **children of Israel**,*

*to a rebellious nation that has **rebelled against Me**. They and their fathers have transgressed against **Me**, to this very day. 4. For they are impudent children and stiff hearted. I AM sending you to them and you will say to them, The word **of Adonai**, the **LORD***. 5. And they, whether they will hear, or whether they will hold back, (for they are a rebellious house) will yet know that there has been a **prophet** among them.*

Ezekiel is immediately transformed into **his** physical body when **he arrives in Israel.**

Ezekiel 2:6. *And you, son of man, **Do not be in awe of them! Do not be in awe of their words!** You are among briers and thorns and you live among scorpions. **Do not be in awe of their words! Do not be dismayed at their looks!** They are a **rebellious** house. 7. And you will speak **My** words to them, whether they will hear or whether they will cease, for they are **most rebellious**.*

*8. But you, son of man, Listen! Obey what I AM says to you! **Do not be rebellious like that rebellious house!** Open your mouth and eat what I AM is giving you. (Rev. 10:9)*

9. And when I looked, behold, a hand was sent to me and, lo, a scroll of a book was there. (Rev. 10:9) 10. And He spread it before me and it was written on both sides and lamentations and mourning and woe were written there. (Rev. 5:1)

Eat the Scroll

Ezekiel 3.1. *Moreover **He** said to me, Son of man, eat what you found. Eat this **scroll** and go **speak** to the **House of Israel**. 2. So I opened my mouth and **He** caused me to **eat** that **scroll**. (Rev. 10:9) 3. And **He** said to me, Son of man, cause your belly to **eat** and **fill** your **belly** with this **scroll** that I give you. Then I **ate** it and in my **mouth** it was as sweet as **honey**. (Rev. 10:9)*

The **LORD*** gives Ezekiel the **Word of God,** the same food we will eat in the Hereafter.

Ezekiel 3:4. *And **He** said to me, Son of man, go to the **House of Israel** and speak to them with **My words**. 5. For you are not sent to a people of an obscure speech and of a hard language, (but) to the **House of Israel**, 6. not to many peoples of an obscure speech and of a hard language, whose words you cannot understand. Surely, had I sent you to them, they would have listened to you. 7. But the **House of Israel** will **not** listen to you, for they will **not** listen to **Me**, for the whole House of Israel is impudent and hard hearted. 8. Behold, I have made your face strong against their faces and your **forehead** strong against their foreheads. 9. I have made your **forehead** like an **adamant** harder than **flint**. Do **not** be in awe of them or be dismayed at their looks, for they are a **rebellious** house.*

Ezekiel is tough against the **Rebellious** Israelites.

Ezekiel 3:10. *Moreover **He** said to me, **Son of man**, take in your heart all **My** words that I shall speak to you and hear with your ears. 11. Then **go**! Come to those of the **captivity**, to the children of your people! Speak to them and tell them, whether they will **listen** or whether they will **not listen**, Thus says Adonai, the **LORD***.*

Notice that this time the LORD* speaks the Scripture to feed Ezekiel. Sometimes in Heaven, we will be fed by eating the Word, other times by hearing the Word.

Ezekiel 3:12. *Then the **Spirit took me up and I heard behind me a great rushing, a voice (saying), Blessed be the Glory of the LORD* from His place**. 13. I also heard the noise of the wings of the **living creatures** that touched one another and the noise of the wheels over against them and a noise of a great rushing. 14. So the **spirit** lifted me up and took me away and I went in bitterness, in the heat of my **spirit**, but the hand of the **LORD*** was strong upon me. 15. Then I came to those of the **captivity** at **Tel Aviv**, **(Babylon)**, who lived by the river of **Chebar** and I sat where they sat and remained there dumbfounded among them seven days.*

*16. And it was at the end of seven days; Then it was the word of the **LORD*** came to me saying, 17. Son of man, I have made you a **watchman** for the **House of Israel**, therefore hear the word from*

My mouth and give them **warning** from **Me**. *18. When I say to the* **wicked**, *You will surely* **die** *and you do not give him warning, nor are you speaking to warn the* **wicked** *from his* **wicked** *way, to save his life. The same* **wicked** *man will die in his* **iniquity**, *but I shall* **require** *his* **blood** *from* **your hand**. *19. Yet if you warn the* **wicked** *and he does* **not** *turn from his* **wickedness** *or from his* **wicked** *way, he will* **die** *in his* **iniquity**, *but* **you** *have* **delivered** *your* **very being**.

Ezekiel was carried in the **Spirit** to the captives at **Tell Aviv, Babylon.** Later his **Spirit** was carried to **Jerusalem** to see the sinful behavior there – while his body was still in **Tel Aviv, Babylon.**

Elijah was **Transformed** as **Elisha** looked on.

2 Kinga 2:11. *And it was, as they still went on and talked that, behold, a* **chariot of fire** *and* **horses of fire** *appeared and divided them both, and* **Elijah** *went up by a* **whirlwind into heaven.** *(Rev. 11:12) 12. And* **Elisha** *saw it and he cried,* **My father. My father!** *The chariot of Israel and its* **horsemen!** *Then he saw him no more and he took hold of his own clothes and tore them in two pieces. 13. He also took up the* **mantle (prayer shawl)** *of* **Elijah** *that fell from him and went back and stood by the bank of the Jordan. 14. And he took the mantle of* **Elijah** *that fell from him and struck the waters and said,* **Where is the LORD* God of Elijah?** *And when he also had struck the waters, they parted here and there and* **Elisha** *went over.*

Verse twelve has the reference to **Father** showing respect; to **chariot** and **horsemen** show **spiritual strength** and **protection.**

Elisha saw the moment of **Elijah's Transformation** into the **Spirit Realm!** The **Horses** and the **Chariot** were **not** physical; the **Fire** was **not** physical. There is **nothing physical** in **Heaven**; **everything** there is **Spiritual**. That means the trees, the water, any animals, all the people, absolutely everything is **Spiritual**!

Y'shua was Transformed as Peter, Jacob, and John watched.

Luke 9:28. *And it was about eight days after these messages, and taking Peter and John and Jacob He went up to the mountain to pray for*

*Himself. 29. And it happened while He was praying, the appearance of His face was different and His **cloak** (was) white, gleaming like lightning. 30. And behold two men were speaking with Him, who were Moses and Elijah, 31. while those who had been seen in glory were speaking about **His death**, which He was going to fulfill in Jerusalem.*

Y'shua's Prayer Shawl changing to gleaming white shows the moment **Y'shua** was **transformed** into the **Spirit Realm**; then **Moses** and **Elijah** were seen **talking** with **Him**, both of them in the **Spirit Realm** too, evidence that **Spirit bodies speak** without vocal cords and **hear** without eardrums. **Moses**, who had died, being in the **Spirit** indicates that other **Saints** could also be given **earthly assignments!** **Elijah** was changed into his **Spirit** body when the flaming **chariot** came for him. Then in Matthew, the **LORD*** **speaks audibly** to a crowd.

Matthew 17:35. *Then a **voice** came from the **cloud** saying, **"This is My Son, the One Who has been chosen, you must continually listen to Him."** 36. And, after the **voice** came, **Y'shua** was found alone. And they kept silent and **no one** reported in those days anything that they had **seen***

In Luke, the same voice speaks from another cloud.

Luke 9:35. *Then a voice came from the cloud saying, "This is **My Son**, the One Who has been chosen, **you must continually listen** to Him."*

Here the **LORD*** again speaks:

2 Peter 1:17. *For then **He** took **honor** and **glory** from **Father God** when such a unique voice announced to **Him** by the **Majestic Glory**, "This is **My Son**, **My Beloved**, with **Whom** I take **delight**," (Matt. 17:5, Mark 9:7, Luke 9:35)*

The **LORD*** honors **Y'shua** at every opportunity in those Scriptures, calling Him **My Son** and saying that **He** takes Delight in **Him**.

Ezekiel was carried to the **Temple** in Jerusalem, so he saw the **Glory of God** fill the **Temple** where **Ezekiel** heard the **LORD*** speaking to him.

Ezekiel 43:5. *So the **spirit took me up and brought me into the inner court** and, behold, the **Glory of the LORD* filled the House**. 6. And I **heard (Him)** speaking to me out of the **House (Temple)** and a **Man** stood by me. 7. And **He** said to me, **Son of man**, the place of **My throne** and the place of the soles of **My feet**, is where **I** and **My holy name** will dwell in the midst of the **children of Israel forever**. The **House of Israel** will no longer defile, they or their kings, by their harlotry or by the carcasses of their kings in their high places. 8. In their setting of their threshold by **My thresholds** and their post by **My posts** and the wall between Me and them, they have even defiled **My holy name** by their abominations that they have committed: therefore **I have consumed them in My anger**. 9. Now they will put away their harlotry and the carcasses of their kings far from Me and **I shall dwell in their midst forever**.*

God, Who is **Spirit**, speaks audibly; God earlier was heard by a crowd.

Matthew 3:17. *And there was a voice from the heavens saying, **"This is My beloved Son, with Whom I am well pleased."***

There will be nearly constant music and singing in Heaven, but there will be at least one period of **Silence!** Various instruments in the **Spirit** are already used in Heaven.

Revelation 8.1. *And when He opened the **seventh seal**, there was **silence in heaven for about half an hour**. 2. And I saw the seven **angels** who stood before God, and seven **trumpets** were given to them.*

The **Trumpets** are **Spirit**! There will be no **silver** and no **gold** in **Heaven**; no **man-made things** are there and will not be there.

The **Gold** of the street in **New Jerusalem** will be **Spiritual**, as all those who attain ETERNAL LIFE will be **Spiritual!**

Revelation 21:21b *And the wide street of the city was pure **gold** like translucent glass.*

The **Glory of God** will shine through the street and from everything in New Jerusalem. The sun will no longer exist and will not be needed because the **Glory of God** will provide light throughout **His Kingdom**. The **Latin text** has the street being **transparent glass**, but the **Greek text** has the street of **translucent glass**. The **Greek** word is **diauges**, which means to **shine through**, as it would with **Translucent Glass**. The **Glory** will light our **entire Heaven**, **shining continuously**, with never any darkness. We will **not** need **sleep** because **worshipping** the **LORD*** will **refresh us**! There will be **No** darkness in Heaven, with everywhere being light from the Glory of God! Everything will shine, glowing with His Glory!

Shofars in Heaven are **Spirit**, not the horns of animals! There will be **no** meat, **no** vegetables, **no** water, **only Spiritual** objects, **Spiritual people**, **Spiritual horses**, **Spiritual buildings**, **Spiritual trees, and grass**. There will be **no brick and mortar** buildings, **no** woven cloth, **no** printed books; everything will be **Spiritual**! Many people want to see their earthly pets in heaven, which may well be, but the pets will be **Spiritual, not physical**. The **people** and any **animals** will be **Spirit, not physical**!

Daniel's Third Vision

> Daniel 10.1. *In the third year (538 BC) of Cyrus king of Persia a thing was revealed to **Daniel**, whose name was called **Belteshazzar**. And the thing was true, but the time appointed was long and he understood the thing, and had understanding of the vision.*

Then Daniel was in something like a trance, and he was instructed by an **Angel**.

> Daniel 10:2. *In those days I, **Daniel**, was mourning **three full weeks**. 3. I **ate no** pleasant bread, neither did flesh or wine enter my mouth, nor did I anoint myself at all, till **three whole weeks** were fulfilled. 4. And on the **twenty-fourth day** of the **first month**, as I was by the side of the **great river**, which is the **Tigris**, 5. then I lifted up my eyes and looked, and behold a **certain man clothed in linen**, whose loins were girded with **fine gold** of Uphaz, (Ufaz). (Rev. 1:13) 6. His **body** also was like the **beryl** and his **face** like the appearance of **lightning** and his **eyes** like **lamps of fire** (Rev. 19:12) and his **arms** and his **feet** like in color to **polished bronze**, (Rev. 2:18) and the sound of his words like the sound of a **multitude**. 7. And I alone, **Daniel**, saw*

*the **vision**, for the **men** who were with me did **not** see the **vision**, but a great quaking fell upon them, so that they fled to hide themselves. 8. Therefore I was left alone and saw this **great vision**, and there remained **no strength** in me, for my comeliness was turned in me into **corruption** and I retained **no strength**. 9. Yet I **heard** the sound of his **words** and when I **heard** the sound of his **words**, then I was in a **deep sleep** on my face, and my face toward the ground. 10. And, behold, a **hand touched me**, which moved me upon my **knees** and the **palms** of my **hands**. 11. And he said to me, O **Daniel**, the man greatly **beloved**, understand the words that I speak to you and stand **upright**, for I am now sent to you. And when he had spoken this word to me, I stood **trembling**. 12. Then he said to me, **Do not be in awe, Daniel!** For from the first day that you **set** your **heart** to understand, and to **chasten yourself** before your **God**, your words were heard and I have come because of your **words**. 13. But the prince of the **kingdom of Persia** withstood me for **twenty-one days**, but lo, **Michael**, one of the chief princes, came to help me and I remained there with the kings of Persia. (Rev. 12:7) 14. Now I have come to make you **understand** what will befall your people in the **latter days**, for yet the vision is for **many days**.*

The **Vision** began at three days after the end of **Passover** and **Unleavened Bread. Visions** outside the Holy Land were usually beside a river; these by the Tigris or the Great River, the Euphrates; Ezekiel's by the Chebar River. In verse twelve, **chasten yourself** means to **fast. Michael** was on earth in the Spirit

Although others were with **Daniel**, they did not see the **Vision,** nor did they hear the **Words** of the Prophecy.

Daniel 10:15. *And when he had spoken such words to me, I set my face toward the ground and I became mute. 16. And, behold, one with the likeness of the **sons of men touched my lips**, then I **opened** my mouth and **spoke** and said to **him** who stood before me, O my **lord**, by the **vision** my sorrows have turned upon me and I have **retained no strength**. 17. For how can the **servant** of this my **lord** talk with this my **lord** for as for me, straightway there **remained no strength** in me, neither is there **breath** left in me. 18. Then one like the **appear-***

*ance of a man came again and **touched** me, and he **strengthened** me 19. and said, O man greatly **beloved**, **Do not be in awe! Peace** be with you! **Be strong!** Yes, **be strong!** And when he had **spoken** to me, I was **strengthened** and said, Let my **lord speak**, for you have **strengthened** me.*

The **angel** strengthened **Daniel,** so **Daniel** was able to converse with the **Angel**. When the **Angel** said, "Peace be with you," he was speaking only to **Daniel** because the word "you" was singular.

The Angel Recaps

Daniel 10:20. *Then he said, Do you **know** why I have come to you? And now I shall **return to fight** with the **prince of Persia**: and when I have gone out, lo, the **prince of Greece** will come. 21. But I shall tell you that which is noted in the **Book of Truth**, and there is no one who holds with me in these things, but **Michael** your **prince**. 11.1. Also I, in the first year of **Darius** the **Mede**, even I stood to **confirm** and to **strengthen** him.*

The **Archangel Michael** had come to tell **Daniel** about the empires that were still to come.

Other Angelic beings come to perform assignments on behalf of men.

The LORD* and two Angels Just Appear beside Abraham.

Genesis 18:1. ***And** the LORD* **appeared** to him in the plains of Mamre and he was sitting in the tent door in the heat of the day. 2. And he lifted up his eyes and looked, and **there were three men standing by him**. And when he saw them, he ran from the tent door to meet them and he bowed toward the ground 3. and said, "My Lord, if now I have found favor in Your sight, do not pass by, I pray You, from Your servant: 4. let a little water, I pray you, be brought and wash your feet and rest yourselves under the tree.*

Abraham was sitting on a hill with a view of the surrounding land because it was from that hill that the LORD* showed him Sodom in the same passage. Notice that the **LORD*** just appeared. That is how **Spirit** travel works!

In verse three, the pronouns You & Your are singular, recognizing God. In verse four, the pronouns are plural, so since ordinary angels are there, "your" is not capitalized.

7
THE SPIRIT REALM IS THREE DIMENSIONAL

That the Spirit Realm is three-dimensional is known from our Glimpses into the Spirit Realm, where we have seen the Third Temple, numerous people, the New Jerusalem, and unique creatures like the four living creatures of Ezekiel. Our best contact with that is with **Y'shua**, Who appeared to many after His resurrection. That gives us a good glimpse at his Spirit Being, Who spoke, heard, saw, and even ate food while with His disciples. Those disciples could touch and see His wounds, even walking a long fourteen-mile round-trip to Emmaus with Peter and Kleopas.

Therefore we, too, will have experiences in the Hereafter that will stretch our imaginations, filling us with Wonder as we marvel at our new surroundings. What we see will be three-dimensional like we are used to seeing, but it will **not** be physical! It will be **REAL,** but **not** physical. Our bodies will **not** be physical, so we will **not** have eyes, but we will see; nor ears, but we will hear; nor noses that breathe, lungs that provide oxygen for our bodies. The Spirit body will not use oxygen! Those who look at us will see each person's teeth, but we will not have physical teeth! Everything will be Spiritual! Although without vocal cords, we will be singing, worshipping the Living God! Without physical eyes, we will see the beautiful scenery of Heaven. Spirit bodies will be complete without being physical. Our communication will be in the Spirit by thought transfer, like speaking in tongues and knowing the interpretation; the person with whom you are speaking may understand what you are saying even if you are thinking in a different language. Without having physical ears, we will still hear! Without vocal cords, we will sing worship and praise to the LORD* and converse with others!

New Jerusalem will be an awesome sight, with the light generated by the **Glory of God**, like the **Light** of **Genesis 1:3**. *And God said, "Light, Be!" And there was light. 4. And God saw the light, that it was good, and God divided the light from the darkness. 5. And God called the **light Day**, and the darkness He called Night. And there was evening and there was morning, **day one**.*

The **Light** was the **Glory of God**! The **Darkness** was there because of the **presence of evil**, later embodied in the serpent.

In the **Hereafter** and in **New Jerusalem** there will be **no darkness**, since everything glows with the **Glory of God**. The streets are **translucent Gold**, glowing continuously. There will be **no shadows** because everything will **glow** with the **Glory of the LORD* and the Lamb** – who are **One**!

Isaiah 60:19. *The sun will no longer be your light by day. Neither will the moon give light to you for brightness, but the **LORD* will be an everlasting Light for you, and your God, your Splendor**. (Rev. 21:23-25) 20. Your **sun will no longer go down nor will your moon withdraw itself**, for the **LORD* will be your everlasting Light**, and the days of your mourning will be ended.*

Revelation 21:22. *And I did not see a **Sanctuary** in it for the **Lord God of Hosts** and the **Lamb** are its **Sanctuary**. 23. And the city has no need of the **sun** or of the **moon**, that they would give light to the city, for the **glory of God**, and the **light of the Lamb**, did illuminate it.*

Our Spirit Bodies will be a radical experience because they will **not** have any physical parts! There will be **no** lungs, **no** hearts, **no** stomachs, **no** intestines, **no** eardrums, **no** bones, **no** joints, and **no** physical hair! We'll have mouths without teeth, although people will see a perfect set of teeth in each one of us! Without ear drums, we will hear Heavenly music and Heavenly Worship! Think about not having muscles, so there will be **no** muscle aches, **no** joint pain, and **no** physical complaints! Without physical brains, we will be absolute whizzes with memorized Scripture! Heaven is Heavenly!

Gone for us will be all the familiar things to which we have become so attached; our **food, phones, cars, TVs, planes, stoves,** and all other **kitchen appliances, clothes, houses,** and a multitude of other things. Our **pets, dogs, cats, fish, parakeets, canaries, and horses,** will not be with us in the flesh. Like us, there will be **horses** in the **Spirit Realm,** but no other animals are named in the Bible to be in the Spirit Realm. The horses will not need hay or oats, corn, and whatever else is in their sweet feed on earth. Listening to Praise and Worship will strengthen them. Perhaps horses will join in the singing, adding their neighing to the chorus.

Will other animals be with us in the Hereafter? Scripture does not give a clue, but God can do anything, so He may well add some other creatures. The only creatures named in Scripture other than Horses are the Living Creatures of Ezekiel.

> Ezekiel 1:4. *And I looked and, behold, a whirlwind came out of the north, a great cloud and a flaming fire and a brightness was around it and out of the midst of it like the color of amber, out of the midst of the fire. 5. Also out of the midst of it was the likeness of* **four living creatures**. *And their* **appearance was the likeness of a man**. *6. And each one had* **four faces** *and* **each one had four wings**. *7. And their feet were straight feet and the* **sole of their feet was like the sole of a calf's foot** *and they sparkled like the color of gleaming bronze. 8. And their* **hands were like a man's** *under their wings on their four sides and the four had their faces and their wings. 9. Their wings were joined one to another. They did not turn when they went, each one going straight forward. 10. As for the likeness of their faces, the four had the face of a man and the face of a lion on the right side. And the four had the face of an ox on the left side. The four also had the face of an eagle. (Rev. 4:7) 11. Thus were their faces, and their wings were stretched upward, two wings of each one were joined one to another and two covered their bodies. 12. And each one went straight forward; they went wherever the spirit was to go. They did not turn when they went. 13. As for the likeness of the* **living creatures**, *their appearance was like burning coals of fire, like the appearance of torches. The fire went up and down among the* **living creatures** *and the fire was bright and lightning went forth out of the fire. 14. And the* **living creatures** *ran and returned like the appearance of a flash of lightning.*

From the **Living Creatures,** we look at what **Y'shua** was doing in His **Spirit** Body:

> John 4:31. *In the meantime the disciples were urging Him saying, "Rabbi, You must now eat." 32. But He said to them, "I have food to eat which you do not know." 33. Therefore the disciples were saying to one another, "Did someone bring Him something to eat?" 34. Y'shua said to them, "**My food is that I would do the will of the One Who sent Me and I would complete His work**.*

Our Spiritual food in Heaven will be **Scripture, Praise, Glory,** and **Honor to God!** But we will be able to eat as Y'shua did in His Resurrected Body. We will all do the Perfect Will of God with every move we make, every thought we think.

> Luke 24:36. *And while they were saying these things He stood in the midst of them and said to them, "**Shalom Aleichem,**" ("**Peace be with you, plural**") 37. But becoming terrified and afraid they were thinking that they saw a **spirit**. 38. Then **He** said to them, "Why are you disturbed and why are the doubts going up in your heart? 39. You must now look at **My** hands and **My** feet because **I AM He**: you must now touch **Me** and see, because a **spirit does not have flesh and bone** just as you see **Me** having." 40. Then having said this **He** showed them **His** hands and feet. 41. But they still did not believe from the joy, and marveling **He** said to them, "Do you have something here to eat?" 42. And they gave **Him a portion of broiled fish**: 43. then after He took it **He ate in front of them**.*

Y'shua's resurrected body was both **physical** and **Spiritual**. Our **Heavenly** bodies will **not** be **physical**, but **only Spirit bodies**. Those bodies will have mouths but no hard enamel teeth; that will not stop us from eating if we are provided with real food! In Heaven, we will not be raising cattle, chickens, fish, and whatever else we eat on earth; there will be **nothing physical** in **Heaven!** The nourishment our spirits need will be provided by the **Word of God!** Our spirits will be refreshed as we sing "**Glory and Honor and Power**" to the Most High God!

Spirit bodies will often be clothed in White Prayer Shawls (Robes of Righteousness), but, like **Y'shua,** we will be able to appear in other clothing.

There will be no fashion shows, no competition, just different outfits for certain assignments.

The Appearance of Y'shua to Miriam Magdalene

Matthew 20:11. *And **Miriam** stood outside at the tomb weeping. Then as she was weeping, she bent over into the tomb 12. and saw **two angels** in white, sitting, one at the head and one at the feet, where the body of **Y'shua** had been lying. 13. And those (**angels**) said to her, "Ma'am, why are you weeping?" She said to them that "They took my Lord, and I do not know where they put Him." 14. After she said these things she turned to those behind and saw **Y'shua** standing but had not recognized that it was **Y'shua**. 15. **Y'shua** said to her, "Ma'am, why are you crying? Whom are you seeking?" Because she **thought that He was the gardener** she said to Him, "Sir, if you removed Him, you must tell me where you carried Him and I shall take Him." 16. **Y'shua** said to her, "**Miriam**." After she turned to that One she said to Him in Hebrew, "Rabbi," which means Teacher. 17. **Y'shua** said to her "Stop touching **Me**, for I have not yet ascended to the Father: you must go to **My** brothers and you must say to them, 'I am ascending to **My Father** and **your Father** and **My God** and **your God.'** 18. **Miriam Magdalene** came and then announced to the disciples that "I **have seen the Lord**," and that **He** said these things to her.*

Y'shua was dressed so that He appeared to be the gardener, showing that it is likely others' **Spiritual Bodies** will be able to appear in different clothes. Then the narrative goes on with White Garments.

Ecclesiastes 9:8. ***Let your garments be always white*** *(Matt. 28:3) and let your head lack no ointment.*

Matthew 28:1. *And after Sabbaths, on the First Day of the Week at dawn, Miriam Magdalene and the other Miriam came to see the tomb. 2. And behold there was a great earthquake: for (there was) an **angel** of the Lord, who descended from heaven, and after he came he rolled the stone away and was sitting upon it. 3. And **his appearance was like lightning and his clothing white as snow**.*

Matthew 17.1. *Then after six days* **Y'shua** *took Peter and Jacob and John his brother and brought them up on a high mountain by themselves. 2. And He was transformed before them, and His face shone like the sun, and* **His garments became white as the light.**

Mark 9:2. *Then after six days* **Y'shua** *took Peter and Jacob and John and led them to a high mountain privately, alone. And He was transformed before them, 3. and* **His garments became shining very white, such as no bleach upon the Earth is able to whiten in this way.**

Luke 9:28. *And it was about eight days after these messages, and taking Peter and John and Jacob* **He** *went up to the mountain to pray for Himself. 29. And it happened while* **He** *was praying, the* **appearance of His face was different and His <u>cloak</u> was white, gleaming like lightning.**

Here, **Y'shua's** garment (**<u>Cloak</u>**) is identified as His **Prayer Shawl**, indicating that people in the Hereafter will be wearing Shining White Prayer Shawls!

Matthew 22:23. *In that day Sadducees, who said there was no resurrection, came to* **Him** *and they asked* **Him** *24. saying, "Teacher, Moses said, 'If someone would die not having children, his brother will marry his wife and he will raise his brother's seed.' (Deut. 25:5) 25. And there were beside us seven brothers: and the first married one died, and since he did not have an heir he left his wife to his brother: 26. then likewise the second and the third until the seventh. 27. And last of all the wife died. 28. Therefore in the resurrection of the seven, whose wife will she be? For they all had her." 29. Then Y'shua said to them, "You are misled, since you do not know either the Scriptures or the power of God: 30. for* **in the resurrection they neither marry nor are given in marriage, but they will be like angels in heaven.** *31. And concerning the resurrection of the dead did you not read what was spoken to you by God saying, 32. 'I AM the God of Abraham and the God of Isaac and the God of Jacob?' (Exod. 3:6)* **He is not the God of the dead but the living."** *33. And when the crowds heard that they were amazed by His teaching.*

And again in Luke:

> Luke 20:27. *And some of the Sadducees came, those who were saying there was not to be a resurrection. They asked Him 28. saying, "Teacher, Moses wrote for us, if some brother would die, if he had a wife, and this one would be childless, that his brother would take the wife and he would raise up a seed for his brother. 29. Then there were seven brothers: and the first, after he took a wife, died childless: 30. then the second 31. and the third took her, and likewise also the seven did not leave a child when they died. 32. Later the wife died also. 33. Therefore the wife, in the resurrection, whose wife does she become? For seven had her as wife." 34. Then Y'shua said to them, "The children of this age are marrying and being given in marriage, 35. and those of that age, and found worthy to* **reach the resurrection of the dead, neither marry nor are given in marriage:** *36. for they are not able to die again, because they are* **like angels and are children of God,** *being children of the resurrection. 37. But since the* **dead are rising,** *and Moses revealed this at the bush, as he said, '***Lord, the God of Abraham and the God of Isaac and the God of Jacob.'** *38. Thus* **He is not the God of the dead** *but of the* **living,** *for* **all** *should be* **living in Him."** *(Exod. 3:6,15,16) 39. Then some of the scribes said, "Teacher, You said well." 40. For they were no longer daring to ask Him anything.*

There will be **no** marriage, **no** living together, **no** mansions, **no** jealousy, **no** contention, **no** strife. We will be with **our families** to a great extent, which we know from so many **kings** going to be with their **fathers** when they **die.** Everyone will have **social** intercourse, **interacting** with **many friends, relatives,** and **new acquaintances.** Just **think** of **making friends** with **famous people of history** and of the **Bible!** Our **conversations** with them will be by **thought transfer** rather than **spoken word,** making **translation unnecessary.**

> Galatians 3:26. *For you are all* **children of God** *through* **faith in Messiah Y'shua:** *27. for as many of you as were* **immersed** *into Messiah, you have been* **clothed** *with* **Messiah.** *28. For there is not one* **Jewish** *or* **Greek,** *not one* **slave** *or* **free,** *there is* **not one male or female.** *For you are all* **one** *in Messiah Y'shua. 29. And if you are*

*of **Messiah**, then you are the **seed of Abraham**, **heirs according to the promise**.*

Many Christians are counting on having a **Mansion** in **Heaven**, but such is **not** to be. The word "**Mansion**" in numerous **Bibles** is there because the first English translations were made from a Latin text, with the Latin word "**Mansiones**" **not** translated, just dropping that next to the last letter **E** for "**Mansions**." The Dictionary of Ecclesiastical Latin **Mansio** is the lexical **word** meaning **Dwelling**, Abode, Home, with no indication of size or appearance. The **Greek** word in John 14:2 is **Monai**, meaning a **staying**, **abiding**; **Y'shua** was speaking about our **Heavenly assignments**, **not promising** anyone a **mansion** in which to enjoy **mint juleps** on the **veranda**. There will be **no brick-and-mortar houses** or any other **brick-and-mortar** buildings. **Heaven** is now and will always be a **Spiritual place** for **Spirit Beings**.

WORDS OF WARNING **NOT** HEEDED

> Jeremiah 36.1. *And it was in the fourth year of Jehoiakim the Son of Josiah king of Judah, this **word** came to **Jeremiah** from the **LORD*** saying, 2. Take for yourself a scroll of a book and write in it all the words that I have spoken to you against **Israel** and against **Judah** and against all the nations from the day I spoke to you, from the days of **Josiah**, even to this day. 3. It may be that the **House of Judah will hear all the evil which I AM thinking to do to them**, so each **man** can **return** from his evil **way** and I shall **forgive** their **iniquity** and their **sin**.*

Iniquity is intentional sin, while **Sin** is unintentional Sin. Each person will be able to **Return – Repent – this being their last chance!**

> Jeremiah 36.4. *So **Jeremiah** called Baruch the son of Neriah and Baruch wrote all the words of the LORD* from the mouth of Jeremiah, which He had spoken to him, upon a scroll of a book. 5. And Jeremiah commanded Baruch saying, I am shut up. I cannot go into the House of the LORD*, 6. therefore you go and read in the scroll, which you have written from my mouth, the words of the LORD* in the ears of the people in the LORD's* House on the fasting day. And you will also*

read them in the ears of all Judah who come from their cities. 7. It may be they will present their supplication before the LORD* and each one will return from his evil way, for great is the anger and the fury that the LORD* has pronounced against this people.

The **Fasting Day** in Verse Six, the son of Neriah did according to all that Jeremiah the prophet commanded him, reading from the scroll the words of the LORD* in the LORD's* house.

Jeremiah 36:9. *And it was in the fifth year of Jehoiakim the son of Josiah king of Judah, in the ninth month, <u>they proclaimed a fast before the LORD* to all the people in Jerusalem</u> and to all the people who came to Jerusalem from the cities of Judah. 10. Then Baruch read the words of Jeremiah from the scroll in the House of the LORD*, in the chamber of Gemariah the son of Shafan the scribe, in the higher court, at the entry of the new gate of the LORD's* House, in the ears of all the people.*

The **Proclaimed Fast** was **not** one of the seven annual fasts honored by Jews.

Jeremiah 36:11. *Now when Micaiah the son of Gemariah, the son of Shafan, had heard all the words of the LORD* out of the scroll, 12. then he went down to the king's house, to the scribe's chamber and, lo, all the princes sat there, Elishama the scribe and Delaiah the son of Shemaiah, and Elnathan the son of Achbor, and Gemariah the son of Shafan, and Zedekiah the son of Hananiah, and all the princes. 13. Then Micaiah declared to them all the words that he had heard when Baruch read the scroll in the ears of the people. 14. Therefore all the princes sent Jehudi the son of Nethaniah, the son of Shelemiah, the son of Cushi, to Baruch saying, Take in your hand the scroll which you have read in the ears of the people and come. So Baruch the son of Neriah took the scroll in his hand and came to them.*

15. And they said to him, Sit down now and read it in our ears. So Baruch read in their ears. 16. Now it was, when they had heard all the words, they turned in fear to one another and said to Baruch, We will surely tell the king about all these words. 17. And they asked Baruch saying, Tell us now, How did you write all these words at his mouth?

18. Then Baruch answered them, He pronounced all these words to me with his mouth and I wrote with ink in the scroll.

*19. Then the princes said to Baruch, Go! Hide yourself, you and Jeremiah and **Do not let anybody know where you are!** 20. And they, the princes, went in to the king in the court and laid up the scroll in the chamber of Elishama the scribe, and told all the words in the ears of the king. 21. So the king sent Jehudi to fetch the scroll and he took it from the chamber of Elishama the scribe. And Jehudi read it in the ears of the king and in the ears of all the princes who stood beside the king. 22. Now the king sat in the winter house in the ninth month and there was a fire on the hearth burning before him. 23. And it was, when Jehudi had read three or four columns, he cut it with the scribes' knife and threw it into the fire that was on the hearth, until the whole scroll was consumed in the fire that was on the hearth.*

The king rejected the Word of the LORD* out of hand. In verse 22, The original Hebrew practice was to number the months and days, not name them. The current name of the month is Kislev, a heathen name given when Israel and Judah were scattered.

*Jeremiah 36:24. Yet they were not afraid, nor did the king or any of his servants who heard all these words tear their garments. 25. And although Elnathan and Delaiah and Gemariah had made intercession to the king that he should not burn the scroll, he would not listen to them. 26. But the king commanded Jerahmeel the son of the king, and Seraiah the son of Azriel, and Shelemiah the son of Abdeel, to **take Baruch** the scribe and **Jeremiah** the prophet, but the **LORD*** hid them.*

*27. Then the **word of the LORD*** came to **Jeremiah**, after the king had burned the scroll and the words which **Baruch** wrote at the mouth of **Jeremiah** saying, 28. Again, take another scroll and write in it all the **former words** that were in the first scroll, which Jehoiakim the king of Judah has burned. 29. And you will say to Jehoiakim king of Judah, Thus says the **LORD***, **You have burned this scroll** saying, Why have you written in it saying, The king of Babylon will certainly come and destroy this land and will cause man and beast to cease from there? 30. Therefore thus **says the LORD*** regarding Jehoiakim king of Judah, **He will have no one to sit on the throne of David and his dead body will be cast out in the day** to the heat and in the* *night to the frost. 31. And **I shall punish him and his seed and his servants for their iniquities a**nd I shall bring all the evil that I have pronounced against them upon them and upon the inhabitants of Jerusalem and upon the men of Judah. But they did not listen.*

Zedekiah Reigns

Jeremiah 37.1. *And king **Zedekiah** the son of **Josiah** reigned instead of **Coniah** the son of **Jehoiakim**, whom Nebuchadrezzar king of Babylon made **king** in the land of **Judah**. 2. But neither he nor his servants nor the people of the land listened to the words of the **LORD***, which He spoke by the prophet **Jeremiah**.*

<u>Coniah</u> is also called Jeconiah and Jehoiakin.

Against Babylon

Jeremiah 50.1. *The word that the **LORD*** spoke against **Babylon** and against the land of the **Chaldeans** by **Jeremiah** the prophet. 2. Declare among the nations! Make it heard! Set up a standard! Make it heard! **Do not hide!** Say, **Babylon is taken!** Bel is shamed! Merodach is broken in pieces! Its idols are shamed, its images are broken in pieces. 3. For out of the north a nation comes up against it, which will make her land desolate, and no one will live there. They will remove, they will depart, both man and beast.*

Restoration of Israel

Jeremiah 50:4. *In those days and in that time, says the **LORD***, the children of **Israel** will come, they and the children of **Judah** together, going and weeping. They will go and **seek** the **LORD*** their God. 5. They will ask the way to **Zion** with their faces toward (Jerusalem saying), Come and let us **join ourselves** to the **LORD*** in a perpetual covenant (that) will **not** be forgotten.*

*6. **My people** have been **lost sheep**. Their **shepherds** have caused them to go astray, they have turned them away on the mountains, they have gone from mountain to hill, they have forgotten their resting place. 7. All who found them have devoured them, and their **adver-***

saries said, **We are not guilty** *because they have* **sinned** *against the* **LORD***, *the* **Habitation of Righteousness**, *the* **LORD***, *the* **hope** *of their* **fathers**.

Medes, Prepare to Take Babylon

Jeremiah 51:11. *Prepare the arrows! Get the shields ready! The LORD* has raised up the spirit of the kings of the Medes, for His device is against Babylon, to destroy it, because it is the vengeance of the LORD*, the vengeance for His Temple. 12. Set up the standard upon the walls of Babylon! Make the watch strong! Set up the watchmen! Prepare the ambushes! For the LORD* has both devised and done that which He spoke against the inhabitants of Babylon. 13. O you who dwell upon many waters, abundant in treasures, your end has come, the measure of your covetousness. (Rev. 17:1) 14. The LORD* of Hosts has sworn by Himself, I shall fill you with men like a swarm of locusts and they will call out against you, Hurrah!*

15. He has made the earth by His power, He has established the world by His wisdom and has stretched out the heavens by His understanding. 16. When He utters His voice, there is a **multitude of waters** *in the heavens and He causes the vapors to ascend from the ends of the earth. He makes lightnings with rain and brings forth the wind out of His treasuries. 17. Every man is stupid in knowledge. Every metal worker is confused by the graven image, for his molten image is falsehood and there is no breath in them.*

The people on earth are not to be in awe of natural storms or what can be done by anyone because we will just transition to our Spirit bodies as we are committed to the **LORD***. **The key to a peaceful lifestyle is devotion to the LORD* and Y'shua!** The two are **One!**

Revelation 22.1. *Then (the angel) showed me a river of water of life, (Torah), bright as crystal, going out from the* **throne** *of* **God** *and the* **Lamb**.

There is **One Throne**, occupied by **God** and the **Lamb**.

Revelation 22:2. *In the middle of its street, also on each side of the river, is a tree of life making twelve fruit, yielding its fruit each month,* *and the leaves of the tree are used for the healing of the multitudes. (Gen. 2:9; 3:22, Ezek. 47:12) 3. And there will no longer be anything there (that is) cursed. And the **throne** of **God** and of the **Lamb** will be in it, and His servants will serve Him 4. and they will see His face, (Ps. 17:15; 42:2) and His **name** (will be) upon their **foreheads.** (Ezek. 9:4, Rev. 7:3; 9:4; 14:1) 5. And there will no longer be night and they will not need the light of a lamp or (the) light of (the) sun, (Zech. 14:7) because the Lord God will give light upon them, and (those **whose names are written in the Lamb's Book of Life**) will **reign** forever and ever.*

The name of God will be "Emet" (Truth) according to the Sohd level of interpretation as done by John in Book Order in Glossary.

*Ezekiel 2:6. And you, son of man, **Do not be in awe of them! Do not be in <u>awe</u> of their words!** You are among briers and thorns and you live among scorpions. **Do not be in <u>awe</u> of their words! Do not be <u>dismayed</u> at their looks!** They are a rebellious house. 7. And you will speak My words to them, whether they will hear or whether they will cease, for they are most rebellious.*

Our Spirit bodies will never be in **awe** or **dismayed**!

*Ezekiel 2:8. But you, son of man, Listen! Obey what I AM says to you! **Do not be <u>rebellious</u> like that <u>rebellious house</u>!** Open your mouth and eat what I AM is giving you. (Rev. 10:9)*

Our **Spirit** bodies will Never be **Rebellious** either!

God's Mercy & Grace

*2 Kings 5:27. Therefore the **leprosy of Naaman** will **cling to you** and to your seed forever. And he went out from his presence a **leper** as white as snow.*

Ezekiel 18:32. For I have no pleasure in the death of the one who dies, says Adonai, the LORD. Therefore **turn** back yourselves, and live!*

Turn and Return are Hebrew idioms meaning to Repent. The Turning is required as a change in behavior needed to be evidence of **Repentance.**

The really **Good News** is John 1:14.

> And the **Word became flesh** and lived among us, and we saw **His** glory, glory in the same manner as the only child of the Father, full of **grace** and **truth**. The **Living Word** came to us to teach us and to show us how we are to **live** by every **Word** from the mouth of **God**, bringing us **eternal life**. 1 Peter 1:18. *Because **Messiah** also once suffered concerning sin, the **righteous One** on behalf of the **unjust**, so that He could bring you to **God** when **He** did indeed die in the flesh, but then was **made alive** by the **Spirit**.*

Y'shua is alive today, having entered that state (**ETERNAL LIFE**) that all of us will enter at the appropriate time.

Another relationship to **Good News** is from three points: **First,** in Genesis 1:27, God made mankind and in verse 31 said it was very good; **Second,** in Genesis 2:23, Adam said Eve was bone of his bones and flesh of his flesh; and **Third** in Genesis 2:24 Adam and Eve became one flesh. That is **Good News** for all mankind, establishing the foundation for Godly marriage, the most important element for Godly living.

8

THE ALLEGORY OF EZEKIEL'S TEMPLE

Ezekiel's Third Temple is a picture of the End of Time and the beginning of the New Jerusalem, with everything physical no longer in existence and everything Spiritual now a Reality. It is not physical, but it is Real!

Water (Torah) Flows from the House

> Ezekiel 47.1. *Afterward* **he** *again brought me to the door of the* **House** *and, behold,* **waters issued from under the threshold of the House eastward**, *for the front of the* **House** *faced the east and the waters came down from under the right side of the* **House**, *at the south side of the* **altar**. *(Rev. 22:1) 2. Then* **he** *brought me out by the way of the gate northward and led me around the way outside to the outer gate by the way that looks eastward and, behold, waters ran out on the right side.*

He is the man with the measuring rod in Ezekiel 40:3. **Water** represents **Torah** in Isaiah 55:1 and Exodus 14:22. The **House** is the **Sanctuary** because the **Altar** is separate from the **House**, so **Water** only flows from the **Sanctuary**, **not** the **Temple**. The **Altar** is in the **Temple**, but not in the **Sanctuary**. The **Water**, the **Sanctuary**, the **Temple**, and the **Altar** are all Spiritual, not Physical, but they are **Real!**

> Ezekiel 47:3. *And when the* **man** *who had the* **line** *in his hand went out eastward, he measured a thousand cubits and he brought me through the* **waters**. *The waters were to the ankles. 4. Again he measured a thousand and brought me through the waters. The waters were*

to the knees. Again he measured a thousand and brought me through. The waters were to the loins. 5. Afterward he measured a thousand and it was a river that I could not cross, for the waters had risen, waters to swim in, a river that could not be crossed. 6. And he said to me, Son of man, have you seen this? Then he brought me, and caused me to return to the bank of the river.

The Water represents **Torah,** so the increasing depth shows us the increasing knowledge of **God's Word** as we live on that **Word** in **Heaven.** The **Word of God** is our Food, our only **Food** in **Heaven!**

Ezekiel 47:7. *Now when I had returned, behold, at the **bank** of the **river** were **very many trees** on the one side and on the other. 8. Then he said to me, These **waters** issue out toward the east country and go down into the **desert** and go into the **sea**. When brought out into the **sea**, the **waters** will be **healed**, 9. And it will be that everything that **lives**, which moves, wherever the **rivers** will come, will **live**, and there will be a very great multitude of **fish**, because these **waters** will come there for they will be **healed** and everything will **live** wherever the **river** comes.*

Heaven is **Spiritual,** so none of the things listed above is physical! There is no **River,** no **Riverbank,** no **Trees,** no **Waters,** no **Desert,** no **Sea.** There will be no **Healing** because every **Sickness** and every **Physical Ailment or disability** will not exist in **Heaven! Heaven** will be occupied by **Spiritual Beings** who have entered **Eternal Life. They will not be Physical,** but they will be **Real!**

Ezekiel 47:10. *And it will be that the **fishermen** will stand upon it from Ein Gedi even to **Ein Eglaim**. There will be a place to spread nets, their **fish** will be according to their kinds, like the **fish** of the **Great Sea**, a great number. 11. But its **miry places** and its **marshes** will not be healed. They will be given to **salt**. 12. And beside the **river**, on its **bank**, on this side and on that side, will grow all **trees for food**, whose **leaf** will not fade, neither will it fail to produce **fruit**. It will bring forth new **fruit** according to its **months**, every **month**, because their **waters** issued out of the **Sanctuary**, and its **fruit** will be for food and its **leaf** for **medicine**. (Rev. 22:2,14)*

This passage is not literal but is an allegory since none of the things listed above will exist in the Hereafter. There will be **no** water, **no** fish, **no** places, **no** marshes, **no** salt, **no** river, **no** trees, **no** fruit, **no** months, **no** food, **no** medicine, and **not anything**! Everything will be **Spiritual**, not **Physical**. It is not possible for a freshwater, inland lake to have salt water swamps on its periphery. These saltwater marshes are an allegory of **Revival**, the source of salt for the people making this is an allegory of revival, with the pure **water** referring to those who take the **Word**; the pockets of salty water, those who do **not take the Word,** who are thrown into the Lake of Fire, the Second Death. All who are in Heaven have **ETERNAL LIFE**.

9

DEATH IS ABOLISHED

Death is the Last Enemy

> 1 Corinthians 15:26. **Death** (is) the **last enemy being abolished**: 27. for "**He subjected all things under His feet.**" (Psalm 8:7) and when He would say that all things have been subjected (it is) clear that the One who subjects all things to (Messiah is Himself) excepted. 28. But when all things would be subject to Him, then also the Son Himself would have been subjected to the One Who subjected all things to Him, so that God would be all in all.

When **Death** is abolished, ETERNAL LIFE is at hand for everyone!

> Isaiah 25:6. And on this mountain the **LORD*** of Hosts will make a **feast** of fat things for all peoples, a feast of wines on the **lees**, of **fat** things full of marrow, of **wines** on well **refined lees**. 7. And on this mountain **He** will **destroy** the face of the **covering** cast over all peoples, and the **veil** that is spread over all nations. 8. **He will destroy death forever** and Adonai, the **LORD***, will **wipe away tears** from **all faces.** (Rev. 7:17) And the **rebuke of His people** will be taken away from the whole earth, for the **LORD*** has spoken it.

Verses six and seven describe the end for Heathens, with the Feast made with fat that looks good, soft and smooth, only it's made from Refined Lees, which are the dregs, having no liquid, but they are dry and bitter, like sawdust. The Covering and Veil represent the protection of God that is now destroyed, removed from the Heathens.

Verse Eight tells of the opposite, the Reward for the Saints, where the LORD Destroys Death Forever, wiping away the tears from each face while removing the scars from the prejudice and hatred against them. Prejudice and Hatred are now, as you read this, sweeping the world, but know that at the end of Judgment Day all believers will be vindicated!

> *1 Corinthians 15:50. But I say this, brothers, that flesh and blood are not able to inherit (the) Kingdom of God, nor does corruption inherit incorruption. 51. Behold I am telling you a mystery: we will not all be asleep (in death), but we will all be transformed, 52. in a moment, in a twinkling of an eye, at the **last shofar**: for a **shofar** will sound and the **dead** will be raised **incorruptible** and we will be **transformed**. (Isaiah 26:19, Dan. 12:13, Rev. 20:5) 53. For it is necessary to clothe this corruptible (with the) incorruptible and to clothe this mortal (with the) immortal. 54. And when this mortal will be clothed immortal and this corruptible will be clothed incorruptible then the written word will happen,*

> *"**Death was swallowed up in victory.**" (Isaiah 25:8)*

> *55. Where, O **Death**, (is) your victory?*

> *Where, O **Death**, (is) your sting?" (<u>Hosea 13:14</u>)*

> *56. But **sin** (is) the sting of **death**, and the power of sin (is taken from) the **Torah** (Teaching): 57. but thanks to **God**, to the **One** Who gives us **victory** through our **Lord Y'shua Messiah**. 58. Thus, my beloved brothers, you must continually be steadfast, immovable, abounding in the work of the Lord always, since you have known that your labor is not without result in (the) **Lord**.*

Death is swallowed up in Victory! Isaiah 21:8 Then the **sting** is removed from it, making **ETERNAL LIFE** the rule for those who have dedicated themselves to the **LORD***.

Hosea, as quoted by Paul, brings yet another confirmation of the wiping out of **Death**.

With the elimination of **Death**, **ETERNAL LIFE** is assured for the **Saints!** So, we will live in the **Spirit Realm** forever, enjoying **LIFE** as we worship the **LORD*** and fellowship with **Saints** and **Kin** forever more! **Life goes on forever!**

So, walk in **Repentance** all day, every day, to be sure you will Enter **ETERNAL LIFE** and never see war, murder, lies, sickness, injury, animal abuse, spousal abuse, child abuse, or any of the many ungodly actions we find all around us in this world.

About the Author

Rev. William J. Morford graduated from Hobart College in 1953 and was a member of the 1955 class of the University of Minnesota's graduate school in hospital administration. Until 1989 Mr. Morford owned and operated a medical administration services company in South Carolina.

He was ordained in August 1988 by Christian International of Santa Rosa Beach, Florida, served on staff as student advisor for Christian International School of Theology and is a Certified Instructor to teach Christian International's series on the prophetic gifts.

From 1993 through 1999, Reverend Morford studied Hebrew under Rabbi Eliezer Ben-Yehuda, grandson of the Eliezer Ben-Yehuda whose lifetime work made Modern Hebrew the national language of Israel.

Reverend Morford and his wife, Gwen have traveled to Israel several times and expect their ministry to take them back for extended periods.

He is the editor of the popular *One New Man Bible* translation and the translator of *The Power New Testament*. He has written nine books; *God's Rhythm of Life, This God We Serve, and One New Man Bible Companion Volumes I - IV, Myths of the Bible, Every Prophet in the Bible, and Glimpses Into the Spirit Realm.*

Please visit ***www.onenewmanbible.com*** to explore the world of the *One New Man Bible.*